Charles Darwin
and the Mystery of Mysteries

By Niles Eldredge
and Susan Pearson

A Neal Porter Book
Roaring Brook Presss

NEW YORK

GREENLAND

ENGLAND

EUROPE

NORTH
AMERICA

NORTH
ATLANTIC
OCEAN

NORTH
PACIFIC
OCEAN

AZORES

CANARY
ISLANDS

AFRICA

CAPE VERDE
ISLANDS

GALAPAGOS
ISLANDS

ASCENSION
ISLAND

SOUTH
AMERICA

BAHIA

ST. HELENA

RIO DE JANEIRO

SOUTH
PACIFIC
OCEAN

VALPARAISO

PAMPAS

SOUTH
ATLANTIC
OCEAN

CHILOÉ

PATAGONIA

MONTEVIDEO

CAPE OF
GOOD HOPE

*From April 1832 to December 1834
the* **Beagle** *sailed up and down along
the coast*

FALKLAND
ISLANDS

STRAIT OF
MAGELLAN

TIERRA DEL FUEGO

CAPE HORN

ANTARCTICA

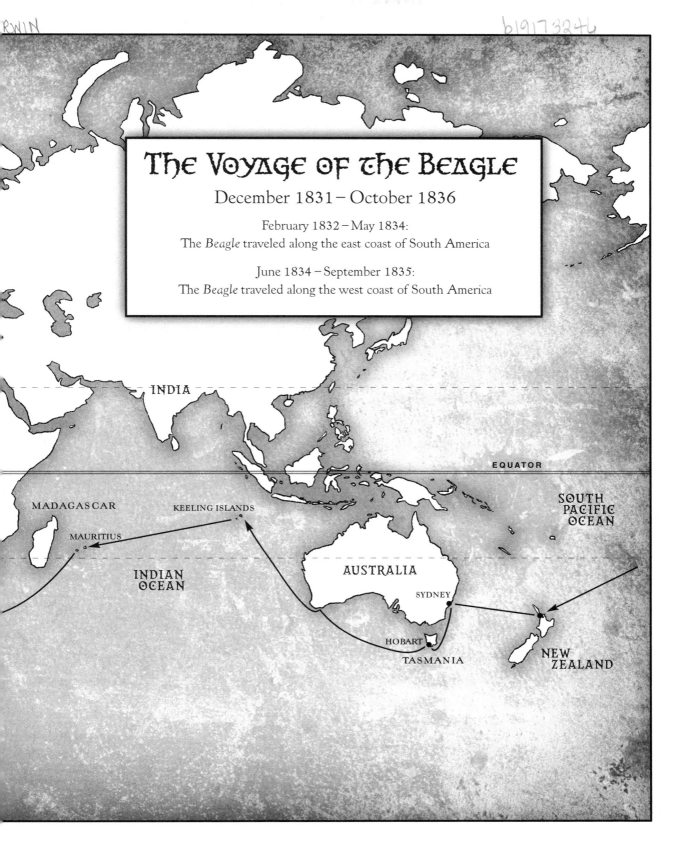

The Voyage of the Beagle

December 1831 – October 1836

February 1832 – May 1834:
The *Beagle* traveled along the east coast of South America

June 1834 – September 1835:
The *Beagle* traveled along the west coast of South America

INDIA

EQUATOR

MADAGASCAR

KEELING ISLANDS

MAURITIUS

INDIAN OCEAN

SOUTH PACIFIC OCEAN

AUSTRALIA

SYDNEY

HOBART

TASMANIA

NEW ZEALAND

A Neal Porter Book
Published by Flash Point, an imprint of Roaring Brook Press
Roaring Brook Press is a division of Holtzbrinck Publishing Holdings Limited Partnership
175 Fifth Avenue, New York, New York 10010
www.roaringbrookpress.com

Designed by Hans Teensma, Impress
Maps by Tim Gabor

Distributed in Canada by H. B. Fenn and Company, Ltd.

Cataloging-in-Publication Data is on file at the Library of Congress.
ISBN: 978-1-59643-374-8

Roaring Brook Press books are available for special promotions and premiums.
For details contact: Director of Special Markets, Holtzbrinck Publishers.

Printed March 2010 in the United States of America
by RR Donelley & Sons Company, Crawfordsville, Indiana
First edition May 2010
2 4 6 8 10 9 7 5 3 1

CONTENTS

vii   FOREWORD

1   A NATURALIST IS BORN

6   SCHOOL DAYS

10   EDINBURGH

16   CAMBRIDGE

22   SUMMER 1831

26   A CURIOUS TURN OF EVENTS

29   UNDER WAY AT LAST

35   CROSSING THE ATLANTIC

39   RIO DE JANEIRO

43   LAND OF THE GIANTS

49   TIERRA DEL FUEGO

53   GALLOPING NORTH

58   EATING THE EVIDENCE

61   THE FUEGIAN EXPERIMENT

64   EXPLOSIONS

68   INTO THE ANDES

71   THE GALAPAGOS

78   SAILING HOME

82   HOME AT LAST

89   FAMILY LIFE AND HUMAN EVOLUTION

97   LIFE AT DOWN HOUSE

103   TRAGEDY

108   A MONTH OF NIGHTMARES

112   *THE ORIGIN OF SPECIES*

119   EPILOGUE

123   TIMELINE OF CHARLES DARWIN ON THE H.M.S. *BEAGLE*

125   TIMELINE OF CHARLES DARWIN'S LIFE AND TIMES

128   NOTES

131   LIST OF ILLUSTRATIONS

132   FURTHER READING

133   INDEX

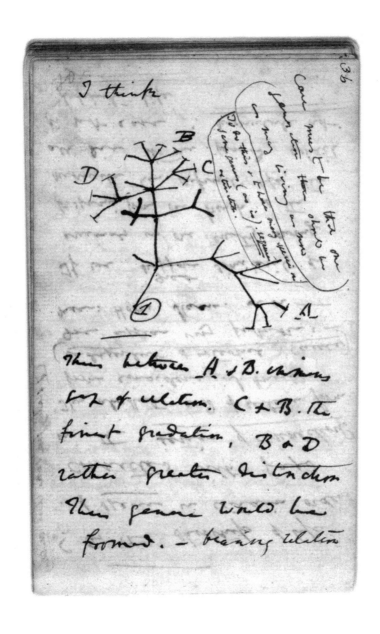

DARWIN'S SKETCH, ON PAGE 36 OF HIS NOTEBOOK B,
OF AN EVOLUTIONARY TREE OF RELATED ORGANISMS

FOREWORD

ALMOST EVERYONE TODAY has heard of Charles Darwin and his theory of evolution. He has been called the most important thinker ever in the history of biology. He has also been called a blasphemer and cartooned as an ape. He was buried alongside kings and queens and England's most honored men and women in London's Westminster Abbey. His face is portrayed with pride on the British ten-pound note. His thoughts about evolution are accepted by scientists around the world. Yet he and his theory are today reviled by many Americans.

What was that theory? Evolution by natural selection: the idea that, through a process of natural selection, all organisms on Earth today have descended from other organisms that existed in the distant past.

Who was this man who created so much controversy? A boy with a passion for collecting bugs. A seasick young man who enthusiastically observed, collected, took notes, and speculated on a voyage around the world. A loving daddy who gleefully bounced his babies on his knee. A patient thinker who painstakingly gathered scientific evidence from all around world. A brilliant scientist with a theory he was afraid to publish.

Charles Darwin was not the first to think of evolution. Though most people of his time (1809–1882) believed that all living species had been created by God within the past 10,000 years and had not changed since their creation, there were a few who suspected that the Earth was much older and that the creatures that had first inhabited it had changed over time, evolving into new creatures. One scientist in particular, the British astronomer John Herschel, wondered when someone would come along to explain what he called the "mystery of mysteries": how extinct species were replaced by new species. That someone would be Charles Darwin, the gentle man many today would call the most controversial scientist in the last two centuries.

CHAPTER 1

A NATURALIST IS BORN

IN THE ENGLAND OF 1809, women's high-waisted dresses and men's ruffled shirts were the fashion, Londoners were just getting used to gas lamps lighting their streets, and canned food was being invented. The Industrial Revolution was under way. New factories and mills and ironworks were popping up around the country, and a spirit of scientific curiosity was in the air. Into this world, on February 12, Charles Robert Darwin was born.

Charles's family was both wealthy and respected. His father, Robert Waring Darwin, was a medical doctor. His mother, Susannah Wedgwood Darwin, was the daughter of Josiah Wedgwood, founder of the famous Wedgwood Pottery, "Potter to Her Majesty." Charles's grandfathers, Erasmus Darwin and Josiah Wedgwood, had been friends for many years. As young men they had gotten together each month with other friends in the neighborhood to discuss philosophy, technology, science, and other interests. Because they traveled to one another's homes by moonlight, they dubbed their group the Lunar Society—members of the club called themselves "Lunaticks." The club included some

IN AMERICA

In 1809, Robert Fulton's steamboat *Clermont* was navigating the Hudson River, Washington Irving was writing "Rip van Winkle," James Madison became the fourth president of the United States, and Abraham Lincoln was born—on the very same day as Charles Darwin.

of England's best and brightest thinkers of the late 1700s. Benjamin Franklin once attended a Lunar Society meeting as a guest.

Charles was the fifth of six children. His oldest sister, Marianne, was eleven when he was born, Caroline was nine, Susan was six, and his only brother, Erasmus, was five. Another sister, Emily Catherine (usually called Catherine), would be born a year later.

The Darwin family lived in a large Georgian house named The Mount in Shrewsbury, the county capital of Shropshire. The town was set on a hillside, at the top of which was a castle, a marketplace, and a school for boys that Charles would later unhappily attend. The Severn River ran around the bottom of the hill on three sides.

JOSIAH WEDGWOOD II, DARWIN'S UNCLE—HIS MOTHER'S BROTHER. "UNCLE JOS" WOULD PLAY AN IMPORTANT ROLE IN DARWIN'S YOUNG LIFE.

WEDGWOOD POTTERY

Wedgwood Pottery was founded in 1759 by Josiah Wedgwood (1730–1795), Charles Darwin's grandfather. By the 1800s, its dinner sets graced the tables of famous homes around the world. Theodore Roosevelt, president of the United States from 1901 to 1909, ordered a Wedgwood dinner service for the White House. Wedgwood continues to manufacture pottery to this day.

This part of the English countryside was as yet untouched by the Industrial Revolution, which was fortunate for Charles, who loved to poke around in fields and meadows. "I was born a naturalist," he once wrote,[1] and he was in the perfect place to develop that inclination.

Being part of the gentry, or gentlemen's class, the Darwins had the luxury of leisure. The family's days were filled with country walks, riding, reading, letter writing, and visits to friends and relatives in nearby towns. Evenings around the fireplace might include discussions of current affairs, politics, art, literature, scientific subjects, and local gossip. Charles's mother and sisters were well read and as likely to participate in these discussions as the men. They entertained, attended plays and balls and concerts, and "rode to hounds" as hunting on horseback was called.

Charles was a dreamy, warm-hearted child who could often be found lying beneath the dining room table reading books like *Robinson Crusoe*, but he spent most of his time outdoors in the woods and fields surrounding Shrewsbury. He had a passion for collecting "all sorts of things,"[2] including shells, stamps, coins, rocks, even eggs. "I was very fond of collecting eggs," he wrote later, "but I never took more than a single egg out of a bird's nest, except on one single occasion, when I took all."[3] He liked to identify whatever plants he came across, and he was especially interested in beetles, which he collected wherever he went. There are more than 250,000 beetle species in the world, and Charles wanted to know every one that lived in England. He kept his collections in a "curiosity cabinet."

Charles loved to fish and spent many hours on the riverbank, but he worried about the pain suffered by the worms he used as bait. He learned that he could kill them more quickly with salt and water, and from then on, he never again fished with living worms, "though at the expense, probably, of some loss of success,"[4] he wrote later.

Though Charles was tenderhearted and rather quiet, there was a streak of mischief in him. "I was in many ways a naughty boy,"[5] he recalled, though his "naughtiness" seems tame by twenty-first century

CURIOSITY CABINETS

Curiosity cabinets are wooden cabinets with many drawers and shelves for storing and displaying collections. They became popular in the 1600s. A traveler's cabinet might have been used to display interesting things picked up on travels to exotic lands, a geologist's cabinet to organize rock samples, or a priest's to showcase religious artifacts. They were a bit like miniature museums.

standards. He was given to making up stories to impress his family and friends. He would often pretend to have seen a rare bird that no one else had spotted, and once he picked the fruit from his father's orchard and hid it in the bushes, "then ran in breathless haste to spread the news that I had discovered a hoard of stolen fruit."[6]   He loved secrets and devised pages of codes which he used to write messages to his little sister Catherine. He had code names for family members and favorite places—Dr. Darwin was "Squirt."[7]

Charles was in awe of his father, a large man about 6 feet 2 inches tall and quite stout. Charles thought him the largest man he'd ever seen. He would later write pages in his autobiography about his father's gift at winning the confidence of others and reading their characters, his extraordinary memory, and his excellent business sense. For his father's part, he was proud of Charles and enjoyed his company

ERASMUS DARWIN

Erasmus Darwin, Charles's paternal grandfather (1731–1802), could aptly be described as "larger than life." He was physically so large that he had a section cut out of his dining table to accommodate his stomach. He had a large mind as well. An abolitionist (as was Josiah Wedgwood), a supporter of women's education, a poet, a philosopher, an inventor, and a physician, he was once asked to be personal physician to King George III, a position he declined.

even when Charles was a very young child. As Charles grew, their interests overlapped, and Dr. Darwin enjoyed sharing his own love of gardening and interest in natural history with his son along with little things about human nature that he had learned in his medical practice.

EARLY EVOLUTIONARY IDEAS

Charles was not the first to have ideas about evolution. His grandfather Erasmus Darwin had written about his own theory of descent in a book, *Zoonomia,* before Charles was even born. A few others had also begun to think that not every species had been created at the same time, but rather that some species might have evolved from others before them. But no one had gathered the factual evidence to support such a theory. No one understood how the evolutionary process actually works. And most people at the time believed that people were not part of this evolutionary process. In fact, they believed that people were not really a part of the animal world at all, but were created by God to rule over it.

JEAN-BAPTISTE LAMARCK

French naturalist Jean-Baptiste de Monet de Lamarck (1744–1829) also believed that species had adapted from earlier species, but he, like Erasmus, did not understand how. Both men thought that traits acquired during a lifetime could be passed on to offspring. If, for example, a cat had to stretch its neck through the bars of its cage in order to reach food—and thus its neck, because of the exercise, grew longer—then it would produce more long-necked cats.[8]

CHAPTER 2

SCHOOL DAYS

I N 1817, WHEN CHARLES WAS EIGHT years old, his mother died. Charles had never known her to be completely well. Throughout his life, Susannah, like many of the Wedgwood family, suffered from chronic illness. (Her brother Tom had died in 1805.) But the summer of 1817, she became so violently ill that it was soon clear to Charles's father that she could not survive. Charles was not allowed to see her while she was so sick, which must have made her death even more difficult for an eight-year-old child to understand.

Charles later wrote that "it is odd that I can remember hardly anything about her except her death-bed, her black velvet gown, and her curiously constructed work-table. I believe that my forgetfulness is partly due to my sisters, owing to their great grief, never being able to speak about her or mention her name; and partly due to her previous invalid state."[1]

This sounds odd to us today—surely an eight-year-old would have *some* memories of his mother. But the family did not gather for meals—like other young children in his social class, Charles and his little sister Catherine had eaten their meals in the nursery—and when his mother was not sick in her room, she was often away from home meeting social obligations. As a young child, Charles wasn't following

CHARLES AT AGE SEVEN,
WITH HIS YOUNGER SISTER,
CATHERINE

his mother around, he was tagging along with his sisters and brother.

Dr. Darwin felt Susannah's loss greatly and never remarried. The older girls also grieved intensely but quickly stepped into the gap to "mother" Charles and his little sister Catherine, on whom they doted. Caroline especially, then sixteen, adored her little brother and became his confidante.

In 1818, just a few months after his mother's death, Charles was sent to Dr. Butler's School in Shrewsbury. Though it was only a little more than a mile from The Mount, he lived at the school day and night except for vacations. His brother Erasmus had started at Dr. Butler's three years before, and it had long been planned for Charles to follow him. In England at that time, most sons of wealthy families left home for boarding school at an early age. There they studied the classics (Greek and Latin languages and literature) in preparation for entrance to Oxford or Cambridge University.

It could't have been easy being sent off to boarding school so soon after his mother's death, but fortunately Erasmus was there. Charles

DR. ROBERT WARING DARWIN,
CHARLES'S FATHER

admired his big brother enormously and would later write in his autobiography about Erasmus's clear mind, extensive knowledge, wit, and kind heart.[2] Their friendship would remain fast throughout their lives.

Despite his brother's presence, Charles hated school. "Nothing could have been worse for the development of my mind than Dr. Butler's school," he later wrote, "as it was strictly classical, nothing else being taught except a little ancient geography and history. The school as a means of education to me was simply a blank."[3]

Charles was much more enthusiastic about less ancient literature—especially the historical plays of Shakespeare and the recently published romantic and swashbuckling poems of Lord Byron and Sir Walter Scott. But these were not part of the "gentleman's education" offered at Dr. Butler's.

In 1819, when Charles was ten, he went to the Welsh coast for three weeks, where he was surprised to find insects he had not found at home in Shropshire. He considered starting a collection of all the insects he could find—but only insects that were already dead, "for on consulting my sister, I concluded that it was not right to kill insects for the sake of making a collection."[4] He also spent hours bird-watching and taking notes on his observations. His enthusiasm for birds was so great he wondered "why every gentleman did not become an ornithologist."[5] Ornithology is the study of birds.

While they were both students at Dr. Butler's school, Ras, as Erasmus was called, set up a chemistry laboratory in the garden shed and allowed Charles to assist him. They analyzed minerals, tea leaves, and whatever else they found interesting and experimented with gases.

Charles's interest in chemistry became known at school, and he was nicknamed "Gas." They were Ras and Gas, the Darwin boys. When Erasmus left Shrewsbury in 1822 to study at Cambridge University, Charles continued their work in the makeshift garden lab.

By the time he was sixteen and coming to the end of his seven years at Dr. Butler's school, Charles had become passionately fond of hunting. For the next several years, he took every opportunity to strike off across the fields with a dog and a gun. His favorite place to hunt was at Maer Hall, his Uncle Josiah (Jos) Wedgwood's Staffordshire estate. Uncle Jos was more easygoing than Dr. Darwin, and he had a special fondness for Charles. His household was relaxed and fun, and with four sons in the family, there was always someone to hunt with; Uncle Jos frequently went, too.

"You care for nothing but shooting, dogs, and rat-catching, and you will be a disgrace to yourself and all your family," Dr. Darwin once told his son.[6]

"When I left the school I was for my age neither high nor low in it;" Charles wrote in his autobiography, "and I believe that I was considered by all my masters and by my Father as a very ordinary boy, rather below the common standard in intellect."[7]

SUSANNAH WEDGWOOD DARWIN, CHARLES'S MOTHER

CHAPTER 3

EDINBURGH

D R. DARWIN HAD HOPES that his sons Erasmus and Charles would follow in his footsteps and study medicine. The doctor was a down-to-earth and kindly man, who believed that often the best remedies were sympathy and talk. He liked to discuss his medical cases with his sons and sometimes even took them with him on his rounds.

When his father had patients whose symptoms weren't serious enough to send them into the hospital, young Charles began "attending some of the poor people, chiefly children and women in Shrewsbury: I wrote down as full an account as I could of the cases with all the symptoms, and read them aloud to my father, who suggested further enquiries, and advised me what medicines to give," he remembered.[1]

Charles liked the work, and his father was pleased.

What Charles *didn't* like was school. His father wasn't totally unsympathetic to Charles's lack of interest in the classics and began to think of removing him from Dr. Butler's School. In 1825, Erasmus was ready to leave Cambridge for medical school in Edinburgh, Scotland. Dr. Darwin decided to send Charles to Edinburgh, too. He was sixteen years old.

◆

SITUATED BETWEEN SEA AND HILLS, the Scottish capital of Edinburgh was full of the excitement of city life. High on the rocks at one end of the city was Edinburgh Castle, the ancient seat of Scottish kings. To the north, between the castle and an inlet from the sea called the Firth of Forth, was the New Town—thousands of classically constructed houses built throughout the 1700s. Below the castle ramparts to the east was the Old Town, teeming with tenement slums, home to thousands of the poor drawn to the city in search of work. At the other end of town from the castle, down a road called the Royal Mile, was the Palace of Holyroodhouse, once the home of Mary, Queen of Scots.

The air of the city was thick with political and religious controversy. Edinburgh was at the forefront of medical discoveries in Europe and alive with scientific, intellectual, and artistic activity.

The university, however, was disappointing to the brothers. Campus buildings begun in their father's day were still unfinished. And most of the students were not of their social rank. Charles and Erasmus were not used to sitting shoulder to shoulder with the sons of "common" men.

The university at that time was full of disorder and conflict. Classes were often rowdy, with students shouting and stomping or using peashooters to signal their approval or disapproval of lecturers. Students were free to choose any course they liked, and professors' salaries primarily consisted of the fees they received from their students. This led to fierce competition among teachers and disrespect on the part of young scholars, who sometimes treated their instructors like hired help.

During their first year, neither Charles nor Erasmus made any new friends. They didn't even join the chemistry society. Instead they spent all of their time together—attending lectures, eating, taking Sunday walks to nearby fishing villages, and collecting shells along the beach. They filled the remainder of their free time with reading.

Charles took the standard courses taken by his father—chemistry, anatomy, surgery, and general medical practice. His anatomy study involved the dissection of human corpses, and Darwin detested it, though he later commented that "it has proved one of the greatest evils in my life that I was not urged to practice dissection, for I should soon have got over my disgust; and the practice would have been invaluable for all my future work."[2]

Darwin's disgust was possibly intensified by stories of the scandalous practices used to obtain bodies for medical labs. By law, only the corpses of convicted criminals could be used for teaching purposes. But there were newspaper reports of grave robbing, and no sensible student cared to be out walking in the Old Town late at night. Indeed, in 1828, a year after Darwin had left Edinburgh, William Burke and William Hare murdered at least sixteen people in order to sell their bodies to the medical school.

Anesthesia had not yet been invented, and surgeries performed at the Edinburgh hospital were hideous to observe. "I saw two very bad operations, one on a child," Darwin wrote, "but I rushed away before they were completed. Nor did I ever attend again, for hardly any inducement would have been strong enough to make me do so; this being long before the blessed days of chloroform. The two cases fairly haunted me for many a long year."[3]

For the rest of his life, Darwin hated the sight of blood.

CHARLES WAS, HOWEVER, ENTHUSIASTIC about his chemistry lectures, which also covered natural history subjects such as geology, mineralogy, and meteorology. They were delivered by a true college character, Thomas Charles Hope. Hope was given to conducting flamboyant demonstrations with spectacular visual effects. Lights flashed. Liquids roiled. Gases swirled. Hope's laboratory equipment was the biggest and the best, but he didn't allow his students to touch it. Students got no lab experience at all in his class, but everyone enjoyed the dramatics.

Around this time Charles met John Edmonstone, a freed slave who worked as a taxidermist for the university's natural history museum. Edmonstone was extremely skilled at reconstructing and preserving the bodies of birds, and Charles hired him to teach him the craft.

LIFE IN THE 1820s

In the 1820s, Noah Webster's American Dictionary of the English Language *was published (1828), Charles Macintosh invented a waterproof fabric that subsequently bore his name (1823), and the game of rugby was originated (1823). The state of Maine entered the Union (1820), the streets of Boston were lit by gas (1822), the Erie Canal was completed (1825), and pianist/composer Frédéric Chopin made his debut in Vienna (1829). In 1821, the population of Great Britain was 20.9 million, the United States 9.6 million, France 30.4 million, and Germany 26 million.*

Charles spent hours working on each specimen, which gave him an intimate understanding of bird anatomy.

By April 1826, when his brother Erasmus finished his medical studies at Edinburgh, Charles had decided that a career in medicine was not for him. But how was he going to tell his father? By summer's end, he had still not broached the subject, so in the fall, back to Edinburgh he went, this time alone.

ERASMUS WAS NOW STUDYING in London at the Great Windmill Street Anatomy School, so Charles, missing the company of his brother, needed to make some friends in Edinburgh. He began to socialize with some of the other students in Robert Jameson's natural history class. Jameson's class was ambitious—some people felt it was too ambitious. It included not only the study of plants, but the study of animals, fossils, and rocks as well. Jameson was world renowned, and his natural history collection was as good as, if not better than, that of the British Museum. He was happy for students to handle his specimens and occasionally took them on field trips as well. Still, after the dramatics of Hope, Darwin found Jameson's presentations dry and disappointing.

In November 1826, Charles joined the Plinian Society, a small group of young men interested in natural history. Named after Gaius Plinius Secundus the Elder (23–79 CE), a noted Roman scholar and naturalist better known as Pliny the Elder, the group met regularly to read and discuss papers on natural science, and occasionally went on collecting expeditions together. One of his fellow Plinians was Robert Grant, who became a good friend.

Charles was still a keen collector of insects, especially beetles, as well as shells, rocks, and minerals. Since he had come to Edinburgh, he had also become interested in the animals living in the seawater of the Firth of Forth—crabs and shrimp, sea anemones, sponges, and other simple forms of marine life. Robert Grant now accompanied Darwin on his Sunday walks to fishing villages, where they explored tide pools and collected sea sponges for study.

Grant taught Charles a great deal about the marine life they collected. He had read of Frenchman Jean-Baptiste Lamarck's ideas about evolution, and he was a fan of Charles's grandfather Erasmus's book *Zoonomia,* which had discussed evolutionary ideas. One day, Charles remembered, Grant "burst forth in high admiration of Lamarck and his views on evolution. I listened in silent astonishment, and as far as I can judge, without any effect on my mind."[4]

THE TITLE PAGE OF ERASMUS DARWIN'S *ZOONOMIA*

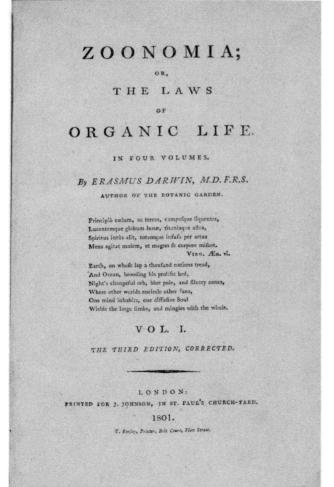

"Grant took me occasionally to the meetings of the Wernerian Society, where various papers on natural history were read, discussed, and afterwards published in the Transactions," Charles later recalled. "I heard [John James] Audubon deliver there some interesting discourses on N. American birds."[5]

Darwin eagerly shared his own observations and discoveries with his friend. But when Grant delivered a paper at the Wernerian Society in which he claimed Darwin's observations as his own, Charles felt betrayed. The friendship was over.

BY THE END OF HIS SECOND YEAR in Edinburgh, Charles knew he had to tell his father that he was not going to become a doctor. By this time he had begun to understand that some day he would be a wealthy man. As he wrote, looking back on his Edinburgh days, he had learned "that my father would leave me property enough to subsist on with some comfort, though I never imagined that I should be so rich a man as I am; but my belief was sufficient to check any strenuous effort to learn medicine."[6] Since he wouldn't have to practice medicine to earn a living, Charles felt he could turn his attention to things he found much more fascinating.

Though his interest in medicine was lost, his interests in collecting, rambling, and shooting were still strong. "My summer vacations during these two years were wholly given up to amusements, though I always had some book in hand," he wrote. "During the summer of 1826, I took a long walking tour with two friends with knapsacks on our backs through North Wales. We walked thirty miles most days, including one day the ascent of Snowdon. . . . The autumns were devoted to shooting, chiefly at Mr. Owen's at Woodhouse, and at my Uncle Jos's, at Maer. My zeal was so great that I used to place my shooting boots open by my bedside when I went to bed, so as not to lose half-a-minute in putting them on in the morning."[7]

And so his days in Edinburgh came to a close.

JOHN JAMES AUDUBON

John James Audubon (1785–1851) was determined to find and paint all the birds of North America. In order to paint them, however, he had to shoot them. He once wrote, "I call birds few when I shoot less than one hundred per day." He then used wires to prop them up in a natural position.

The first to paint birds set in their natural habitat and in real-life positions, he was wildly popular in England, where they called him "The American Woodsman." Even King George IV was a fan. Audubon's book *Birds of North America* is still available today.

CHAPTER 4

CAMBRIDGE

D R. DARWIN WAS NOT PLEASED with his son's decision. If Charles was not to be a doctor, then what was he to be? "He was very properly vehement against my turning [into] an idle sporting man," Charles wrote in his autobiography, "which then seemed my probable destination."[1]

Dr. Darwin decided his son would become a clergyman. Charles asked for some time to think about this, read a few theological books, and, as he "did not then in the least doubt the strict and literal truth of every word in the Bible," agreed.[2]

Studying to be a clergyman meant first taking a degree in the Arts, which included study of the classics. Dr. Darwin decided to send Charles to Cambridge, but since Charles had not opened a classical book since leaving Dr. Butler's—and hadn't cared much for the classics back then—he now found he had forgotten almost everything he had learned there. So his father hired a tutor, and Charles spent the next nine months cramming, though not without breaks to go shooting with Uncle Jos.

CHARLES ARRIVED AT Christ's College, Cambridge, in January 1828. The university then, as now, was made up of many different colleges, of which Christ's College was one. Charles found Cambridge very different from Edinburgh. For one thing, it seemed much calmer than Edinburgh had been. For another, the students of Cambridge came mainly from Charles's own background, so he felt more comfortable. And he was able to make friends right away, thanks to relatives and friends already at Cambridge. One of the best of those friends was a cousin, William Darwin Fox, then in his final year at Christ's College.

Fox was a passionate collector of natural things. His rooms were filled with everything from stuffed swans to incubating cocoons. There were collections everywhere, on every available surface, and more stuffed into hampers in the cellar. Fox also enjoyed shooting and riding and kept two dogs with him at Cambridge. Here was a companion made to order for Charles!

Though Darwin and Fox were only at Cambridge together for six months, during that time they became fast friends. Every day they attended lectures until 10 a.m., then met for breakfast in Fox's rooms. Often other friends would join them for good food and lively talk. After breakfast, the rest of the day was theirs until the formal evening dinner in the college hall.

Charles attended lectures haphazardly. He was more likely to be found hunting, riding, or hiking the countryside with friends. His circle of friends had grown wide. From one, he developed an appreciation of art and engravings. Others were musicians, and Charles grew passionate about music. He often timed his walks so as to pass by King's College Chapel when the choir was singing—the music, he said, made chills run up his spine.[3]

But more than anything else, Charles was passionate about collecting insects. He had loved bugs as a boy, and he loved them still as a young man. It was a passion his cousin William shared. "No pursuit at Cambridge was followed with nearly so much eagerness or gave me so much pleasure as collecting beetles," Charles wrote.[4] He was so wrapped up in beetle collecting that a friend, Albert Way, cartooned him riding a giant beetle, captioning his sketch "Go it Charlie!"

Today a collector of bugs usually carries along a field guide that

DARWIN'S TIN EAR

Although Darwin so enjoyed music that he sometimes hired choir boys to sing in his rooms, he could not keep time or even hum a tune correctly. This was a great source of amusement for his friends, who would tease him by playing a tune faster or slower than usual. No matter how familiar the tune was in its regular beat, when it was played at a different pace, Charles couldn't recognize it.[8]

identifies the various species and subspecies. But in 1828 no such field guides existed. At that time, very little was known about native British insects, so it was possible for Darwin and Fox to actually add to the world's body of knowledge by finding new species or new information about already known species. The cousins spent hours searching for insects in fields and marshes, under fallen leaves, inside dead logs, then studying them, comparing them, and exchanging them with other collectors. "I am dying by inches from not having any body to talk to about insects," Darwin wrote Fox when the holidays came around and they were separated for a few weeks.[5]

Darwin's enthusiasm was legendary. "One day, on tearing off some old bark, I saw two rare beetles and seized one in each hand," he wrote, "then I saw a third and new kind, which I could not bear to lose, so that I popped the one which I held in my right hand into my mouth. Alas it ejected some intensely acrid fluid, which burnt my tongue so that I was forced to spit the beetle out, which was lost, as well as the third one." [6]

In the winter, Charles hired a man to scrape moss off old trees and collect rubbish at the bottom of barges that had brought reeds from the lowlands outside of Cambridge, "and thus I got some very rare species," he wrote. "No poet ever felt more delight at seeing his first poem published than I did at seeing in Stephen's *Illustrations of British Insects* the magic words, 'captured by C. Darwin, Esq.' "[7] The beetle Charles had caught was *Blethisa multipunctata.*

Darwin and Fox were not alone in their enthusiasm for the natural world. They were young men of their time. Natural history was becoming a hugely popular pastime in England, with amateurs and experts alike collecting fossils, shells, rocks, plants, *anything* natural, sometimes keeping them in private collections, sometimes using them to decorate household objects, sometimes sharing them with the scientific community. Collecting from nature was becoming a national fever.

Darwin's college classes consisted of mathematics, geometry, algebra, theology, and Latin and Greek, but he later wrote that "during the three years which I spent at Cambridge my time was wasted, as far as the academical studies were concerned, as completely as at Edinburgh and at school."[9] When his thoughts were not about the natural world, they were about shooting, for which his enthusiasm never waned, and while at Cambridge, he kept an elaborate notebook recording everything he had shot.

But the "circumstance which influenced my whole career more than any other," reflected Darwin, "was my friendship with Professor Henslow."[10]

John Stevens Henslow was professor of botany at Cambridge. Before that, he had been professor of mineralogy. In 1828, when Darwin entered Cambridge one month shy of nineteen, Henslow was thirty-two years old, at the height of his university career, and one of the most respected men in his field.

Henslow was a botanist—a person who studies plants. He became an expert in the plants of Great Britain (England, Wales, Scotland, and Ireland) and would later found the Cambridge Botanical Garden. He was a pioneer in the study of how plants vary from place to place— a key to Charles's later ideas about evolution. A careful collector, John Henslow taught his students to be careful as well—to protect their specimens and keep rigorous notes. His was the only natural science class Darwin took while at Cambridge.

THE FIRST FIELD GUIDES

In the 1820s and 30s, many new natural history magazines began to appear. They got their information from ordinary people who, like Charles Darwin and William Fox, collected "curiosities." The magazines then published lists of species for other collectors to use as guides.

CARTOON OF CHARLES DARWIN RIDING AN ENORMOUS BEETLE, DRAWN BY HIS FRIEND ALBERT WAY AND CAPTIONED "GO IT CHARLIE!"

Henslow's lectures were packed with other professors as well as students. In addition to the lectures, field trips were frequent—sometimes on foot, sometimes by coach, sometimes by barge. As the group traveled, Henslow would lecture happily on whatever they happened to pass, be it plant, animal, insect, fossil, or mineral. Sometimes the day would end with a meal at a local inn, more talk, and often singing.

Each spring a group of about twenty (including some wives and sisters, as well as students and professors) would travel twenty miles west of Cambridge to Gamlingay heath, where they rambled with Henslow in search of unusual specimens. In the evening, they had rooms at a local inn, where they dined to the music of a band hired for the occasion. These trips were remembered fondly by everyone on them, including Charles Darwin.

In 1828, Henslow began hosting weekly Friday evening gatherings of ten or fifteen people in his home to discuss science. Henslow had collected an impressive assortment of specimens, and it wasn't unusual to find a skull or a claw on the table next to you. He encouraged his guests, who included famous men as well as students, to bring along their own finds as well. Mrs. Henslow served tea.

Through his cousin William Fox, Darwin was invited to attend these evenings. "Before long I became well acquainted with Henslow," Charles wrote, "and during the latter half of my time at Cambridge took long walks with him on most days; so that I was called by some of the dons [professors] 'the man who walks with Henslow'; and in the evening I was very often asked to join his family dinner."[11]

THE REVEREND JOHN STEVENS HENSLOW

DARWIN'S ADMIRATION for Henslow lasted all his life. "His knowledge was great in botany, etymology, chemistry, mineralogy, and geology," Charles wrote many years later. "His moral qualities were in every way admirable. He was free from every tinge of vanity or other petty feeling; and I never saw a man who thought so little about himself or his own concerns."[12]

The discussions at Henslow's Friday evenings were enormously stimulating to Darwin. There he was, a young man of twenty, listening to and talking with some of the great natural science minds of the day. They encouraged him to read Sir John Herschel's *Introduction to the Study of Natural Philosophy*, which, along with Alexander von Humboldt's *Personal Narrative*, stirred in him "a burning zeal to add even the most humble contribution to the noble structure of Natural Science."[13]

The Friday night group also discussed theology. Charles Darwin had, after all, entered Cambridge to become a clergyman. Like many university dons of the time, John Henslow was also an Anglican priest. Along with John Herschel and his fellow Cambridge science professor, the Reverend Adam Sedgwick, Henslow believed that science was intimately connected to God's truths. In essence, because nature was the work of God, natural science was the study of God's work.

THE BEGINNING OF PROFESSIONAL SCIENCE

In the early 1800s, when Darwin was young, there were no professional scientists as we know them. Today we have thousands of scientists working in universities, museums, and industry throughout the world. But in Darwin's time, most scientists were either people who had enough money to support themselves without working at a full-time job, or they were educated members of the clergy, working at universities or in local churches where they preached to their congregations every Sunday. Much of the best natural history study in the first half of the nineteenth century was done by clergymen like Adam Sedgwick and John Stevens Henslow.

STUDENT LIFE IN 1828

If it sounds as if Charles Darwin didn't spend much time at Cambridge actually studying, that's because he didn't. This, however, was not unusual for college students of the day, who often spent most of their time hunting, fishing, socializing, even touring Europe, then cramming before their exams. Since before 1829 students were not tested at all until their final exams, the young "scholars" had a great deal of time to enjoy themselves.

CHAPTER 5

SUMMER 1831

CHARLES DARWIN sincerely believed he would eventually become a clergyman. Perhaps one day he, like Henslow, would teach at the university. But in the meantime, he longed to travel.

In *Personal Narratives*, a book that had excited Henslow's Friday evening discussions and seized Darwin's imagination, Alexander von Humboldt had written of his expedition into the Brazilian rain forest. Humboldt eloquently described the thick jungles teeming with life and the magnificent views from the Andes Mountains. He theorized about the great scientific questions of the time and even contemplated artistic and philosophical issues. The book was downright inspirational.

Humboldt had also written about the island of Tenerife in the Canary Islands, off the Atlantic coast of northern Africa, which he described as a scientific paradise. There he had climbed to the top of *el Pico del Teide*, Tenerife's 12,200-foot volcano. He described how the island's plant life descended in layers, each of them suited to its specific soil, water, and elevation—grasses on top, then tall flowering shrubs, then pines, then hardwood trees amidst thick ferns, and finally tropical plants such as date palms and figs at the bottom. He marveled at an ancient 60-foot dragon tree and wondered, since it was native to the West Indies and never grew wild in Africa, how it had gotten there.[1]

Charles grew passionate about traveling to Tenerife and following in Humboldt's footsteps. He would fit the trip in after graduation, before returning to Cambridge to study for the clergy. Several of his friends, including Henslow, were interested in joining him, though Henslow's other commitments, including a new baby, prevented his inclusion.

Charles prepared for the trip in a fever of excitement. Tenerife was a volcanic island complete with white pumice ash like snow on its mountaintops. Humboldt had speculated that not only the ash but the evening hazes and even the plant life were all due to the volcanic origins of the island.[2] Henslow, a former professor of mineralogy himself, insisted that in order to understand what he would be seeing, Charles needed a better knowledge of geology.

Unfortunately, when Charles went to make passenger ship bookings in July, he discovered that ships only traveled to the Canary Islands in June. Charles didn't give up; he just postponed the trip until next year.

That was no reason to postpone his geologic education, though. Eager that Charles learn as much as he could about geology before making the Tenerife trip, Henslow asked his friend Adam Sedgwick, geology professor at Cambridge, if he would take Darwin with him on his annual field trip. In August 1831, Sedgwick was heading to North Wales, where he would be working on refining and correcting the national geologic map and looking for fossils. He agreed to take Darwin along.

At the time, Charles did not know Sedgwick well and had never attended any of his lectures. "Had I done so," he later wrote, "I should probably have become a geologist earlier than I did."[3] He had, however, no doubt spoken with Sedgwick at Henslow's Friday evenings, and had certainly heard of his equestrian field days. Leading sixty or seventy students on horseback, Sedgwick would gallop through the countryside around Cambridge, stopping at prearranged points to observe the geology of

TENERIFE IS THE LARGEST OF THE CANARY ISLANDS. TODAY IT IS A POPULAR TOURIST DESTINATION.

the area and winding up at some inn for dinner and merriment.[4]

Adam Sedgwick was a highly respected geologist, elected president of the Geological Society of London in 1829 and again in 1830. He occasionally hiked in the Lake District with the poet William Wordsworth. Another poet, Alfred Tennyson, had been one of his students.

Enthusiastic, energetic, dedicated to his field of study, Sedgwick believed that all nature reflected the goodness of God, and he was passionate about rocks. He believed they could explain the world's history, perhaps even reveal God's purpose.

As Darwin's home in Shrewsbury was on the way to his destination in Wales, Sedgwick spent the night of August 4 with the Darwin family at The Mount. Charles enthusiastically scoured the geologic sites in the neighborhood before Sedgwick arrived and was excited to tell him that a worker in a nearby gravel pit had found a large tropical shell in the pit. To Charles's disappointment, Sedgwick was not impressed and "at once said (no doubt truly) that it must have been thrown away by someone."[5] Sedgwick went on to explain that had a tropical shell truly been found in the middle of England, it would overthrow everything then known about geology.

Years later, Charles would write that "nothing before had ever made me thoroughly realize . . . that science consists in grouping facts so that general laws or conclusions may be drawn from them."[6] The scientific process, Charles now believed, was a process of gathering many, many facts. Only then, based on all the facts, could a theory be drawn.

Though Charles would travel with him for only about a week, Sedgwick was an enthusiastic teacher. He led Charles to fossil sites and

THE REVEREND ADAM SEDGWICK

explained the significance of the fossils, he taught him how to recognize rock formations and make field drawings, and he lectured about stratification and other geologic phenomena. Charles began to see the Earth through a geologist's eyes. He learned that the layers at the bottom of a series of strata are the oldest. He looked at how wind and rain have worn away rocks to see how the Earth has changed over time. He searched for clues in the rocks that might show the results of old earthquakes and volcanic eruptions, even of the building up and tearing down of older mountains.

Darwin began to think of himself as first and foremost a geologist. "Tell Prof. Sedgwick he does not know how much I am indebted to him for the Welch expedition," he later wrote to Henslow. "It has given me an interest in geology, which I would not give up for any consideration." [7]

At Capel Curig, a village in Conway County, North Wales, Charles left Sedgwick and set off with his compass and a map across the mountains to Barmouth, "never following any track unless it coincided with my course. I thus came on some strange places and enjoyed much this manner of traveling." At Barmouth, he joined some friends for a time, then returned to Shrewsbury for some shooting, "for at that time I should have thought myself mad to give up the first days of partridge-shooting for geology or any other science." [8]

CHAPTER 6

A CURIOUS TURN OF EVENTS

CHARLES'S PLAN was to return to Cambridge in the fall, complete his studies to become a clergyman, travel to Tenerife in the Canary Islands the following June, then return home to take up his duties as a minister. But when he returned home from his summer travels, he found a letter from Henslow informing him "that Captain FitzRoy was willing to give up part of his own cabin to any young man who would volunteer to go with him without pay as a naturalist"[1] on the next voyage of the naval ship *Beagle*.

In 1831, maps of the world were still being revised and there remained many areas, both on land and sea, that had not yet been fully explored. For both economic and political reasons, Britain wanted to know more about the coastal waters of South America, and the *Beagle*'s mission was to chart them. The voyage was expected to last two years, and Captain FitzRoy, just four years older than Charles, did not look forward to the loneliness of the journey. There were plenty of others on board, of course, but they were all his subordinates. He was looking for someone he could talk with.

Charles was eager to accept, but his father, concerned that his son would never settle down and that the whole scheme was basically useless anyway, strongly objected. So Charles "wrote that evening and refused the offer."[2] The next morning, disappointed, Charles went off to Maer Hall to go shooting with his Uncle Josiah. Before he left, though, Dr. Darwin had second thoughts. "If you can find any man of common sense, who advises you to go, I will give my consent," he told Charles,[3] who understood immediately that by "any man of common sense," his father meant Uncle Jos. To make matters even clearer, Dr. Darwin wrote a note to his brother-in-law saying that if Josiah thought the trip a good idea, Dr. Darwin would follow his advice.

Uncle Jos thought the voyage was such a good idea that he immediately wrote a letter to Dr. Darwin in which he gave detailed responses to each of his objections. Dr. Darwin then not only consented, but agreed to finance Charles's trip as well.

On September 1, 1831, Charles accepted the offer to accompany Captain FitzRoy on the voyage of the *Beagle*. "Next day," he wrote, "I started for Cambridge to see Henslow, and thence to London."[4] Armed with letters of introduction from Henslow, Charles scurried around London, getting the counsel of prominent naturalists on what equipment to buy and what he might expect to see. He purchased books, instruments (including a portable dissecting microscope, a telescope, a compass, a device to measure rainfall, and a barometer), a net to catch sea life from the rear of the ship, notebooks, pens and pencils, a geological hammer for breaking rocks and prying specimens out of the ground, and jars in which to preserve the specimens in alcohol. He sent urgent requests home for shirts and shoes. And finally, Charles met Captain FitzRoy.

The captain had had some second thoughts about inviting a perfect stranger on so long a voyage, but the meeting went well. Darwin was impressed by the young seafarer, and, more important, FitzRoy liked Darwin. In the end, Darwin wasn't given a place on the *Beagle* because he was a great naturalist or because he was a great scholar, but because he was of the right social class and looked like he'd be pleasant to have around.[5]

DR. DARWIN'S OBJECTIONS

In order for his uncle to respond, Charles made a list of his father's objections to the trip:

• *Disreputable to my character as a Clergyman hereafter*
• *A wild scheme*
• *That they must have offered to many others before me, the place of Naturalist*
• *And from its not being accepted there must be some serious objection to the vessel or expedition*
• *That I should never settle down to a steady life hereafter*
• *That my accommodations would be most uncomfortable*
• *That you should consider it as again changing my profession*
• *That it would be a useless undertaking*[6]

CAPTAIN ROBERT FITZROY

Robert FitzRoy was just twenty-six years old in 1831. In his autobiography, Charles described him as "devoted to his duty, generous to a fault, bold, determined, indomitably energetic," handsome, and with the fine manners of a gentleman. However, he added, "FitzRoy's temper was a most unfortunate one." [8] His temper was usually worst in the mornings, when he could generally find something wrong on the ship and someone to blame for it.

FitzRoy did not think of himself as a cruel captain, and by the standards of the time, he wasn't. He did, however, believe that order had to be kept, and lashings with a cat-o'-nine-tails would make sure that it was. He was always most kind to Darwin; it was his crew who experienced the pain of his wrath.

After the successful meeting with FitzRoy, Charles spent a few weeks in Shrewsbury with his father and sisters. Then, on October 24, he moved to Plymouth, where the *Beagle* would depart. And there he waited. The weeks stretched on while Captain FitzRoy refitted the ship. When preparations were finally complete, they were held back by bad weather. Weeks became months.

In the port of Plymouth, Charles was often included in FitzRoy's social engagements. He occasionally dined with the captain, and he became acquainted with one of his cabinmates, John Lort Stokes, who taught him how to use his scientific equipment. Nevertheless, Darwin later said that those months of waiting were the most miserable he ever spent. Not only was he feeling lonely for family and friends, he developed worrisome physical symptoms. There was a rash around his mouth, and his heart had begun to beat wildly. That, combined with chest pains, convinced him that he must have heart disease. He did not consult a doctor, however, since, as he later recalled, "I fully expected to hear the verdict that I was not fit for the voyage, and I was resolved to go at all hazards." [7]

The months of misery came to an end at last. On December 27, 1831, the *Beagle* left the shores of England with Charles aboard.

CAPTAIN ROBERT FITZROY

CHAPTER 7

UNDER WAY
AT LAST

ONLY NINETY FEET LONG and twenty-four feet wide at its middle, the *Beagle* was not a large ship. It had three masts and only two cabins. You could easily fit eighteen *Beagles* onto a football field. Despite its small size, it was carrying seventy-four people: the captain, his crew, an artist, an instrument maker, a volunteer missionary, Charles, and three Fuegians.

On his earlier *Beagle* voyage, Captain FitzRoy had taken a small girl and three young men away from their families in Tierra del Fuego at the southern tip of South America, stowing them on board and eventually bringing them all the way back to England. There he outfitted them in English clothing and put them into a village school just outside London. The young Fuegians had quickly learned English and picked up English manners so well that FitzRoy was able to show them off to the king and queen as his "successful experiment." One had died of smallpox, but the other three had survived, and now that his experiment was finished, he was taking them back to Tierra del Fuego.

The cabin that Charles would be sharing with two others was just eleven feet long and ten feet wide. Charles had to duck to enter it. His cabinmates were two of the survey officers—John Lort Stokes, whom he had gotten to know in Plymouth, and fourteen-year-old Midshipman Philip Gidley King. Stokes was responsible for redrafting the navigational charts. The charts were stowed in lockers along the cabin's wall alongside about a hundred books, one of which was Volume I of *Principles of Geology* by Charles Lyell, a gift from Captain FitzRoy. Professor Henslow had recommended it with the advice that Charles shouldn't believe everything in it.[1] Stokes's drafting table took up the rest of the space. At night, Darwin and King hung their hammocks above the table. Stokes slept in a bunk beneath the stairs outside the door.

The *Beagle* was supposed to stop first at Madeira, where ships often took on fresh food, but the sea was rough and Captain FitzRoy decided to head instead for Tenerife—the very island Charles had been so excited to visit the previous summer. Charles was too sick to care.

Throughout the five-year voyage, he would be seasick nearly every day the *Beagle* was under way. In spite of that, he wrote to his father in February, "I find to my great surprise that a ship is singularly comfortable for all sorts of work.— Everything is so close at hand. . . . If it was not for sea-sickness the whole world would be sailors."[2]

FitzRoy thought Charles might well leave the ship at Tenerife and not continue on the voyage. If Darwin elected to remain on Tenerife, not only would he avoid more seasickness, he would be in the "scientific paradise" Humboldt had so eloquently described.

But around the time of the *Beagle*'s departure, there had been outbreaks of cholera in a number of English cities. The officials on Tenerife insisted that the *Beagle* remain in the harbor for twelve days' quarantine before anyone would be allowed to disembark. This FitzRoy was unwilling to do, and so they sailed on. Darwin's spirits sank as he watched the place he had most set his heart on slowly sink into the horizon.

SÃO TIAGO (SANTIAGO) IS THE LARGEST ISLAND OF CAPE VERDE AND THE FIRST TO HAVE BEEN SETTLED.

CHARLES LYELL AND
PRINCIPLES OF GEOLOGY

Charles Lyell was initially trained as a lawyer, but by 1830 he was a full-time geologist. *Principles of Geology*, his first book, was published in three volumes from 1830 to 1833. It was the most influential geological book of its time. In it Lyell argued that the geological Earth we see today was shaped very slowly over a very long period of time, and that changes in the Earth are still going on today. This theory was called "uniformitarianism," and it was in direct opposition to the common thought of the time that everything had been created, just as it is today, all at once in the ancient past or by processes in the past that no longer occur. In 1848, Lyell would be knighted for his geological work.

SIR CHARLES LYELL

Instead of Tenerife, the *Beagle* stopped at the island of St. Jago, now called São Tiago, one of the Cape Verde Islands about 300 miles off the northwest coast of Africa. "The neighborhood of Porto Praya," where they anchored, "viewed from the sea, wears a desolate aspect," wrote Darwin in his journal,[3] but inland, tropical life abounded—palm trees, fruit trees, lush green vegetation, birds, butterflies, even wild cats. His seasickness forgotten, Darwin was in a collecting fever: he found brightly colored sponges, tropical corals, sea slugs, and other life in the pools below the coastal cliffs, even an octopus. But it wasn't long before geologic thoughts filled his mind.

"The geology of this island is the most interesting part of its natural history," he wrote. "On entering the harbour, a perfectly horizontal white band, in the face of the sea cliff, may be seen running for some miles along the coast, and at the height of about 45 feet above the water."[4] What could have caused the strange white stripe? Charles was determined to figure it out, and within two days he thought he had the answer.

When he examined the streak at close range, Charles found numerous shells in it—the same shells that he also found on the beach. Beneath the streak were volcanic rocks. Above it was a stream of basalt—lava cooled off and hardened into rock—which, Darwin deduced, "must have entered the sea when the white shelly bed was lying at the bottom."[5] He concluded that molten lava must have fallen into the sea, baking the shells on the sea floor into a hard white rock. Then the sea bottom had to have been pushed up out of the sea by underwater volcanic activity,

DRAWINGS OF THE H.M.S. *BEAGLE*. THE SHIP WAS ONLY NINETY FEET LONG AND TWENTY-FOUR FEET WIDE AT ITS WIDEST PLACE.

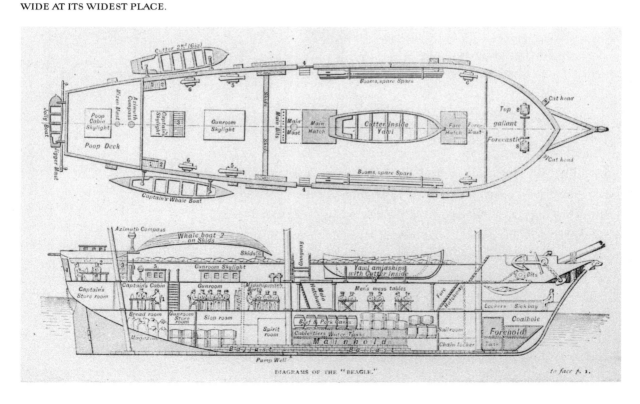

THE *BEAGLE*'S MISSION

The *Beagle* was a British naval ship. On this trip it was under the supervision of the Hydrographer's Office. (Hydrography is the description and study of bodies of water.) Its primary job was to survey the southern coast of South America. But it also had many other assignments, including conducting a number of scientific studies, delivering mail to colonists, setting up an Anglican mission, and exploring as much of Tierra del Fuego as possible.

The British were interested in the riches of South America. They wanted to know everything they could in order to set up military and commercial bases there. But they weren't the only ones. The French, the Russians, the Germans, and even other British ships were all exploring the area at the same time as the *Beagle*. The seas were busy indeed!

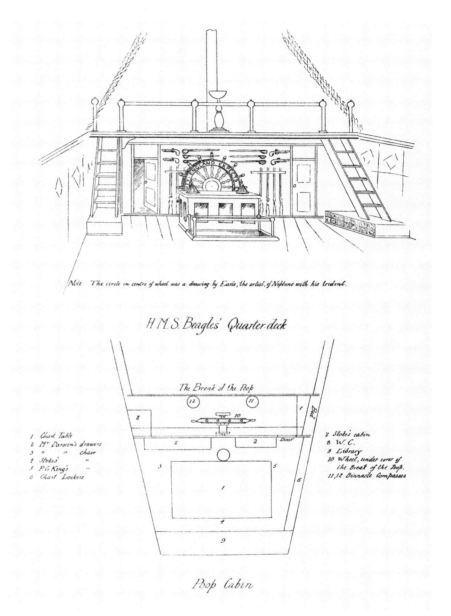

Note The circle in centre of wheel was a drawing by Earle, the artist, of Neptune with his trident.

H.M.S. Beagles' Quarter deck

The Break of the Poop

1 Chart Table
2 Mr Darwin's drawers
3   „   „   chair
4 Stokes'   „
5 P.G King's   „
6 Chart Lockers

7 Stokes' cabin
8 W.C.
9 Library
10 Wheel, under cover of the Break of the Poop.
11,12 Binnacle Compasses

Poop Cabin

TOP: THE POOP DECK OF THE BEAGLE SHOWING THE DOOR INTO DARWIN'S CABIN
BOTTOM: A FLOOR PLAN OF DARWIN'S CABIN. AT NIGHT HE SLEPT IN A HAMMOCK HUNG OVER THE TABLE.

creating this island with its streaked sea cliff. Because the shells in the rock were the same as the shells on the beach, all this could not have happened too long ago geologically.

This was an amazing conclusion to have come to in 1832. It was the correct one, but it flew in the face of Jameson, Henslow, *and* Sedgwick— all of Charles's teachers—who each believed that volcanic islands had all been made in the ancient past. Charles had been reading Lyell's *Principles of Geology* and, though he had not yet finished the book, already it was influencing his scientific thinking. One of Lyell's main points was that as much geologic activity is happening today as was happening thousands of years ago, and that the rate of geologic activity does not vary much over time.

Charles was more excited than he had ever been in his life. Already he was beginning to contribute to scientific knowledge. He was also beginning to understand the power of his own mind. He would remember this moment for the rest of his life.

A KEEN OBSERVER

Since childhood, Charles Darwin had been a keen observer of the natural world around him. His powers of observation grew even more precise as an adult. Here, for example, is what he wrote in his journal about a São Tiago sea slug:

During our stay, I observed the habits of some marine animals. A large Apylsia is very common. This sea-slug is about 5 inches long; and is of a dirty yellowish colour, veined with purple. At the anterior extremity [its front], it has two pairs of feelers; the upper ones of which resemble in shape the ears of a quadruped [four-footed animal]. On each side of the lower surface, or foot, there is a broad membrane, which appears sometimes to act as a ventilator, in causing a current of water to flow over the dorsal branchiae [gills]. It feeds on delicate seaweeds, which grow among the stones in muddy and shallow water; and I found in its stomach several small pebbles, as in the gizzards of birds. This slug, when disturbed, emits a very fine purplish-red fluid, which stains the water for the space of a foot around. Besides this means of defence, an acrid secretion, which is spread over its body, causes a sharp, stinging sensation, similar to that produced by the Physalia, or Portuguese man-of-war. [6]

CHAPTER 8

CROSSING THE ATLANTIC

L EAVING SÃO TIAGO, the *Beagle* sailed southwest toward
Bahia (today called Salvador), Brazil. Darwin began to follow a
daily shipboard routine that would continue throughout the
voyage. After breakfast with Captain FitzRoy, Charles spent his mornings at work. He might be found sharing the giant table in his cabin
with Stokes, studying specimens under his microscope, drying
them, preserving them, sometimes dissecting them, drawing
them, labeling them, numbering them, and writing notes
about them while Stokes worked on his maps and charts.
Or he might be on deck, pulling in the net he had hung
from the rear of the ship to examine the night's catch,
observing the birds in the sky and small organisms called
plankton in the water, and taking notes on everything.

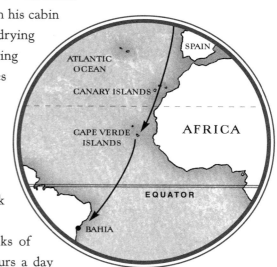

Midday dinner was usually with the captain, then back
to work.

Sea captains were required to keep detailed logbooks of
daily events aboard ship, and FitzRoy spent several hours a day

DARWIN'S NOTEBOOKS

Today we think of Charles Darwin as a biologist, but while he was traveling with the *Beagle*, he thought of himself primarily as a geologist. During the five years of the trip, he made 1,383 pages of notes about geology and only 368 pages about animals. These notes filled several books. On the way home, Charles would begin to mull over his considerable data, and by the time he returned to England, he had already planned several books on geology and zoology.[3]

working on his. Darwin began to keep a logbook too. In fact, he eventually kept two of them—one for geological, the other for zoological and botanical observations. In his geological log, he kept notes about landforms, mountains, rocks, and soil. His zoological and botanical logbook was full of entries about animals and plants. He also kept a personal diary. And he regularly wrote long letters home, sometimes enclosing bits of his diary. On top of that, he kept field notebooks of observations made on the spot.

This endless note-taking would serve him well when the time came to draw conclusions from all his observations.

It was a time-honored custom that when mariners crossed the equator for the first time, they had to be initiated. Charles was one of the thirty-two who were in for it. Even Captain FitzRoy got into the act, dressing up as Neptune, the ancient Greek god of the sea. Charles's face was lathered with tar and "shaved" with a rough piece of iron. Blindfolded, he was doused in a sail filled with seawater. Everyone, the captain included, got thoroughly soaked.[1]

After two short stops, the first on February 16 at St. Paul's Rocks about 540 miles off the South American coast, the second on February 20 at the island of Fernando de Noronha, the *Beagle* dropped anchor at the port of Bahia, Brazil, two months after setting sail.

Here at last were the rich tropical rain forests that Darwin had read about in Humboldt's *Personal Narrative*. On February 29, Charles wrote excitedly about his first day wandering by himself in a Brazilian forest. "The elegance of the grasses . . . the beauty of the flowers, the glossy green of the foliage,"[2] the loud hum of the insects, even getting caught in a tropical storm—all delighted him.

The city of Bahia, however, did not please him at all.

Bahia was a pretty Portuguese colonial city that bragged about its 365 churches—one for every day of the year. Its wealthy citizens lived on a hill high above the city. Beneath them, at the base of the cliff, lay the docks, full of the smells of rotten fruit and the bustle of a busy seaport. Nearly all the work there was done by black slaves. Darwin was outraged.

Charles had been raised to be opposed to slavery. His grandfather Josiah Wedgwood had been active in the Committee for the Abolition of the Slave Trade back in the 1780s and 90s. He had even designed an anti-slavery cameo that showed a chained slave beneath the phrase, "Am I not a man and a brother?" Charles's other grandfather, the first Erasmus Darwin, was also an outspoken abolitionist. And Charles knew personally from his own friendship with the taxidermist John Edmonstone that a black man was no different from any other man.

In Brazil, Darwin heard terrible stories of masters abusing their slaves. One day he heard a slave owner threaten to sell all his slave women and children away from their husbands and fathers. Charles was horrified and said so to Captain FitzRoy.

FitzRoy, however, did not share Darwin's anger. Most wealthy European families had paid servants. To FitzRoy's mind, slavery wasn't all that different. And besides, FitzRoy thought, Africans were inferior to Europeans and less able to take care of themselves. They were actually happy to be slaves. FitzRoy told Darwin he was certain of this. He had asked a local slave owner about it. The owner had called his slaves

"CROSSING THE EQUATOR ON THE *BEAGLE*" BY AUGUSTUS EARLE, ONE OF THE TWO ARTISTS ON THE VOYAGE

before him and asked if they would rather be free. No, they had said.

Darwin was shocked. Just what did FitzRoy *think* the slaves were going to say? How could they answer anything else with their master standing in front of them?

FitzRoy exploded. In 1832, the captain was absolute master of his ship. *No one* contradicted him. How dare Darwin doubt his word about slavery or anything else? He ordered

Charles out of his cabin. He could not dine with such an insolent man!

But FitzRoy's fury passed quickly. He sent an apology to Darwin later that afternoon. Charles did not change FitzRoy's mind, nor did he back down from his own beliefs about slavery. But from then on, he kept those beliefs to himself—at least around Captain FitzRoy.

CHAPTER 9

RIO DE JANEIRO

FROM BAHIA, the *Beagle* sailed south to Rio de Janeiro. For the next few months, from April to July of 1832, the ship would sail up and down the coast of Brazil, checking the charts and correcting the maps. Darwin was not needed on board, so he disembarked, happy to have firm ground under his feet again. Augustus Earle, the ship's artist, and Philip King joined him.

Earle had been in Rio before and was eager to show the others the town. The streets were filled with elegant hotels, ornate churches, wealthy ladies in gleaming carriages, and, to Darwin's dismay, thousands of black slaves.

A few days after their arrival, Charles met an Englishman who was traveling to his estate about a hundred miles away. He invited Charles to join him. Charles happily agreed. The trip, however, took them through the heart of slave country. Over and over, Darwin was horrified at how badly black people were treated.

When he returned to Rio, he rented a cottage at Botafogo Bay, a few miles outside of the city. There he happily scoured the rain forest, gathered specimens, and made scientific notes for the rest of his stay. It was as if Charles had arrived in heaven. After one trip into the forest, he wrote, "At this elevation the landscape has attained its most brilliant

FIREFLIES

Charles Darwin was mistaken in his conclusion that fireflies stay illuminated. Their illumination is caused by a chemical reaction in their light-producing organs and is used primarily in courtship, though at least one species imitates the mating flashes of other species in order to attract and then eat them. Some fireflies synchronize their flashes, a phenomenon that can be seen in the United States in the Great Smoky Mountains near Elkmont, Tennessee. Day-flying fireflies do not produce light at all.

tint; and every form, every shade, so completely surpasses in magnificence all that the European has ever beheld in his own country, that he knows not how to express his feelings."[1] He raved about the flowers and marveled at the insects. On a single day he found sixty-eight different species of beetle! He wrote to Professor Henslow that the beetle specialists in England should begin sharpening their pencils, they would have so much work to do describing these new species when his specimens reached them. "I am at present red-hot with Spiders," he continued, "they are very interesting, & if I am not mistaken, I have already taken some new genera.—I shall have a large box to send very soon to Cambridge."[2]

"It was impossible to wish for any thing more delightful than thus to spend some weeks in so magnificent a country," he wrote in his journal.[3]

His cottage was located at the foot of Corcovado Mountain. It was a place of particular beauty, and the weather during May and June, which was autumn in Rio de Janeiro, was ideal. During the warm evenings, Charles found it "delicious to sit quietly in the garden and watch the evening pass into night."[4] Frogs chirped, cicadas and crickets "kept up a ceaseless shrill cry,"[5] fireflies winked on and off. Charles caught several fireflies and studied them. He noted that their light came from two abdominal rings. The front ring lit up first. When he decapitated an insect, its rings remained lit, though not as brightly as before. One firefly's rings stayed lit for twenty-four hours after its death. Darwin concluded that the firefly could only turn its light off for short periods, that its normal condition was glowing, and that it stayed illuminated automatically.[6] This time he was mistaken.

ONE DAY AN OLD PORTUGUESE PRIEST he had befriended took Charles hunting in the nearby forest. The priest set his dogs loose, and the men sat around waiting for the dogs to flush some game from the brush. Charles found such inactivity boring. He was much more interested in the worms he found. They were a kind of planarian flatworm. All the planaria then known lived in water, and Charles was surprised to find these on dry land. Charles spent his "hunting" day gathering specimens for study.

He took the worms back to the cabin and measured them. He examined them under his microscope. He consulted reference books. He cut them in half and watched them grow into two whole worms. He dissected them. He felt certain that these flatworms were planaria, even though they were not water dwellers, and he wrote to Henslow about his discovery. Henslow was doubtful.[7] But Darwin felt sure he was right. For the remainder of the voyage, he would search for flatworms. In the end he found at least eight species of land-dwelling planaria.[8] Henslow and Darwin would continue to companionably argue the point for many years.

In another forest, he was delighted by a beetle. The bug was attracted to a smelly fungus Charles was carrying. Charles remembered

similar beetles in England that were attracted to a similar smelly English fungus. "We here see in two distant countries a similar relation between plants and insects of the same families, though the species of both are different," he noted.[9]

THE BEAGLE REACHED MONTEVIDEO ON JULY 26, 1832.

On the morning of July 5, 1832, the *Beagle* left Rio de Janeiro with Darwin aboard. Sailing south, the ship reached Montevideo at the mouth of the Río de la Plata (Plata River) on July 26. Across the water was the city of Buenos Aires, Argentina. For the next two years, the *Beagle* would be busy surveying the southern coastline of South America. Darwin would have plenty of opportunities to leave the ship and explore inland, and he would take full advantage of those opportunities. In fact, during the five years of the voyage of the *Beagle*, Charles spent two-thirds of his time on land exploring and collecting specimens. By the end of the trip, he had collected specimens of more than 1,500 different species. Hundreds of them had never been seen before in Europe.[10]

SENDING STUFF HOME

Throughout his journey, Darwin was shipping things home. Crates filled with specimens went off to Henslow, and letters went back and forth between Charles and his family, his friends, Professor Henslow, and other colleagues back in England. A batch of letters was awaiting Charles when he arrived in Rio, and future letters from home would be sent to ports where it was known the *Beagle* would stop.

Darwin's shipments were valuable. First of all, his specimens had scientific value. Their study could lead to new discoveries. They could change current scientific thought and help to identify new species. Papers would be written about them. New species would be named—often for the collector. Second, the British were mad for collections. They flocked to public displays of collections of all kinds. Museums and zoos were opening to satisfy some of that public interest. And finally, though Darwin had no intention of selling his specimens, had he been interested, he could have gotten a very good price for them.

CHAPTER 10

LAND OF THE GIANTS

THE SEAPORT OF BAHÍA BLANCA overlooks the Atlantic Ocean about 350 miles southwest of Montevideo and Buenos Aires. It was the last major outpost before the wild land of Patagonia stretched out to the south. In 1832, there were violent struggles over these lands. Spanish cattle ranchers were at war with the natives. Troops of soldiers led by a rancher called General Juan Manuel Rosas rampaged through the territory, massacring entire native families. Rosas commanded his own army and eventually overthrew the government of Buenos Aires to install himself as governor in 1835.

The atmosphere of violence made Darwin cautious as he set out on his explorations, but he was not really part of these struggles, and life in the wild outdoors suited him. Just as he had loved hunting in the British countryside, now he loved riding across the pampas (prairie) hunting for game. And he was good at it. He often rode out with a crew sent by Captain FitzRoy to find dinner, and he was known as a fine marksman. He even learned to use the bola—a leather thong about eight feet long, at each end of which was a round stone covered with

leather. Charles had admired many a mounted gaucho (cowboy) galloping at breakneck speed, holding one ball in his hand, whirling the other
above his head, then flinging it at his running prey. The thong tangled
around the animal's legs and brought it down. Darwin was eager to
master the art himself.

"One day, as I was amusing myself by galloping and whirling the
balls round my head, by accident the free one struck a bush," Charles
recalled. "It immediately fell to the ground, and like magic caught one
hind leg of my horse. . . . The Gauchos roared with laughter; they cried
they had seen every sort of animal caught, but had never before seen a
man caught by himself."[1]

Of course, Darwin didn't hunt only for meat. He hunted for specimens. Interesting bugs, reptiles, and mammals were everywhere.

CAPYBARAS

THE SOUTH AMERICAN RHEA

Sailors of Darwin's time usually called the rhea an ostrich, which it resembles, though ostriches are taller. The greater rhea is about 5 feet tall and weighs forty-five to fifty-five pounds. It has gray or gray-brown feathers and large wings, but like the ostrich, the rhea cannot fly.

Scientists wondered for years whether or not the rhea and the ostrich are directly related. Today scientists believe the rhea and the ostrich, as well as other ostrichlike birds, are descended from a single ancestor that lived on the large land mass of Pangaea, which later broke into the separate continents we know today.

JOHN GOULD'S RENDERING OF "DARWIN'S RHEA"

Rodents were especially numerous, and Charles eagerly collected eight different kinds of mice. One of his prizes was a giant *Hydrochoerus hydrochaeris*, or capybara, the largest gnawing animal in the world. It weighed ninety-eight pounds and was the size of a St. Bernard dog.[2] The capybaras at Maldonado were very tame—Charles was able to walk within three yards of some. When seen from a distance, they looked like pigs, and they grunted a bit like pigs as well. But close up they looked more ratlike. Despite the fact that capybaras are currently farmed for food, Darwin felt they were better for studying than for dinner; the taste of their meat was, Charles said, "very indifferent."[3]

Charles loved stalking birds, especially strange varieties he had never seen before. On one morning walk alone, he bagged eighty different species.[4]

A bird that particularly caught Darwin's fancy was the ostrichlike South American rhea. Rhea eggs were delicious, as was rhea meat, and Charles soon learned to take the big birds down with a bola. He was puzzled to find some rhea eggs scattered seemingly willy-nilly about the pampas while others were collected in shallow ground nests. The gauchos explained that the male rheas build the nests. Females then come along and lay their eggs—some in the nest, others on the ground in the area. The males roll some of those scattered around into their nests and leave the rest where they lie. The males then hatch the eggs in the nests and care for the chicks.[5]

BY AUGUST 1832, Captain FitzRoy's fit of anger a few months earlier was long forgotten. In a letter to the Admiralty's Office on August 15, he wrote, "Mr. Darwin is a very superior young man,—and the very best (as far as I can judge) that could have been selected for the task.— He has a mixture of necessary qualities which makes him feel at home, and happy, and makes every one his friend."[6]

In September 1832, Charles and Captain FitzRoy were out exploring the bay around Bahía Blanca in a small boat. They were passing the cliffs of a headland called Punta Alta when they noticed some broken bones sticking out of the rocks. Were they fossils? They quickly beached the boat and went to explore. Indeed they were fossils. With the help of some of the *Beagle*'s crew, Charles spent the next week digging large teeth, huge bones, and giant jaws out of the cliff. In all, Charles uncovered the partial skeletons of three big animals and a giant skull of another, as well as numerous small bones of local species.

Charles found a section of bony plates forming the shell from the back of an extinct giant mammal. He excitedly wrote to Professor Henslow that he thought they must belong to an enormous extinct species of Armadillo. Living armadillos were very common—Charles had eaten them for dinner and thought they were delicious. He knew that they had very few teeth, or none at all, in the front of their mouths. Scientists had already classified them together in a group of mammals they called *edentates*, meaning "lacking teeth." The bones Charles had dug out of the cliff seemed to belong to this group.

There was some confusion about what kind of extinct animal actually wore that bony coat of armor. Charles could not wait to hear the analysis from expert Richard Owen back in London. He spread the bones out on the deck of the *Beagle*, carefully labeled and packed them, then shipped them back to England. It wasn't until Owen had finally analyzed the specimens, after Darwin had already arrived back home, that Charles's first hunch was confirmed: he had stumbled on the fossilized remains of a gigantic extinct species of armadillo.

There is no evidence from his letters home that he was thinking yet about evolution, but the clues were starting to appear. In the case of the giant armadillo, *why*, Darwin would soon wonder, did it go extinct? And *why* was it replaced by a similar but smaller species—a species that

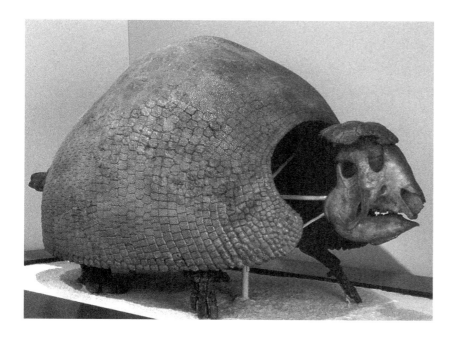

A FOSSIL GLYPTOTHERIUM, RELATED TO THE MODERN ARMADILLO

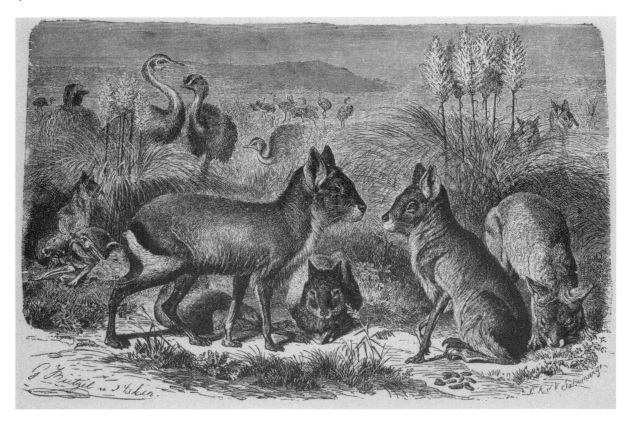

A PATAGONIAN TABLEAU
WITH RHEAS AND CAVIES

lived in this one place and nowhere else in the world?

In October 1832, the *Beagle* returned to Buenos Aires and Monte-video. There they took on provisions before setting sail for Tierra del Fuego, a group of islands at the southernmost tip of the continent.

CHAPTER 11

TIERRA DEL FUEGO

MONG THE *BEAGLE*'S PASSENGERS were three of the four Fuegians, natives of Tierra del Fuego, whom Captain FitzRoy had brought back to England with him on a previous voyage. One had died, but the captain was returning the other three to their homeland. He had named the girl Fuegia Basket and the two young men York Minster and Jemmy Button.

The practice of bringing "sample" natives back to England for show was not uncommon. It had been the captain's idea to "civilize" the Fuegians, then return them to Tierra del Fuego where they would in turn civilize their people. He had felt perfectly entitled to take them. While he had them, he would baptize them as Christians, which he considered his duty.

FitzRoy planned to set up a mission while in Tierra del Fuego. The Church Missionary Society had agreed to furnish supplies, and had also raised money to pay a young missionary, Richard Matthews, to stay on the island and teach the natives how to farm, build houses, clothe themselves properly according to English standards, and speak

TIERRA DEL FUEGO

"Tierra del Fuego may be described as a mountainous country, partly submerged in the sea, so that deep islets and bays occupy the place where valleys should exist," Charles Darwin wrote. "The mountain sides (except on the exposed western coast) are covered from the water's edge upwards by one great forest ... succeeded by a band of peat, with minute alpine plants; and this again is succeeded by the line of perpetual snow." [1]

TIERRA DEL FUEGO LIES AT THE SOUTHERNMOST POINT OF SOUTH AMERICA, SEPARATED FROM THE CONTINENT BY THE STRAIT OF MAGELLAN.

English. Matthews would also instruct them in the Anglican faith. Fuegia Basket, York Minster, and Jemmy Button were expected to help the missionary bring "civilization" to their people.

Darwin had gotten acquainted with the three Fuegians during the voyage and did not think of them as any different from anyone else. He thought Fuegia Basket "a nice, reserved young girl, with a rather pleasing but sometimes sullen expression, and very quick in learning anything, especially languages."[2] To Charles, not only African slaves but all people on Earth, no matter how primitive they might seem, were essentially the same. They might look a bit different and have different traditions, but underneath they were all human beings.

But Charles was startled when he first saw the native countrymen of the Fuegians he had come to know. "As we passed under one cliff, four or five men suddenly appeared above us, forming the most wild and savage group that can be imagined," he wrote in his journal. "They were absolutely naked, with long streaming hair; and with ragged staffs in their hands: springing from the ground they waved their arms around their heads, and sent forth most hideous yells."[3] Tierra del Fuego is a harsh land of snow-covered mountains, giant glaciers, and freezing temperatures, which made the men's nakedness even more amazing to the coat-clad Englishmen.

Captain FitzRoy chose Woollya Cove, where Jemmy Button had lived, as the site for his mission to the Fuegians. But the joyous reunion FitzRoy had anticipated for Jemmy and his family was a terrible disappointment. Jemmy had forgotten his native language and was barely interested in his family. Nor did they seem to find Jemmy's return a cause for celebration.

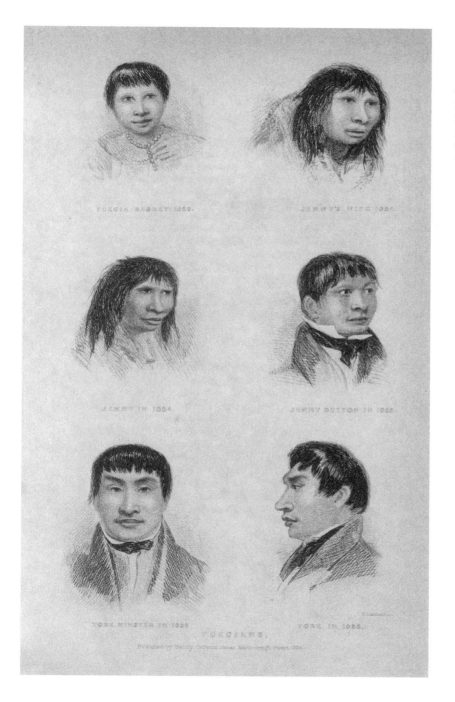

THE FUEGIANS WHO TRAVELED
HOME ON THE *BEAGLE*: FUEGIA
BASKET *(TOP)*, JEMMY BUTTON
(MIDDLE), AND YORK MINSTER
(BOTTOM), SKETCHED BY
CAPTAIN ROBERT FITZROY

FitzRoy set up his mission in January 1833. But when they opened the crates packed by the Missionary Society, they found wine glasses, china dishes, linen napkins, gentlemen's top hats—all sorts of things an upperclass English gentleman might want in his home. There was nothing the missionary Richard Matthews would ever need in Tierra del Fuego.

The Fuegian men watched while the Fuegian women helped the crew build wooden wigwams, fence in two gardens, and plant crops.[4] Apparently the Fuegians did not consider such work suitable for men.

With the mission structures built, the sailors returned to the *Beagle* and sailed on to continue surveying the coastline. When they returned a few weeks later, Matthews ran, screaming, to the captain's launch. He refused to go ashore again. Clearly Tierra del Fuego was not proving to be a place welcoming to English missionaries.[5]

ANOTHER NATIVE KIDNAPPING

The Pilgrims probably would not have survived their first winter in the New World without the help of Squanto. A Pawtuxet Indian, Squanto had been kidnapped by Captain George Weymouth in 1605. He was taken back to England, where he learned English, and eventually returned to America in 1614 with Captain John Smith. He was then kidnapped again and taken to Spain. He finally returned home in 1619 only to find that the entire Pawtuxet tribe had been wiped out in a plague in 1617.

On March 22, 1621, the Pilgrims met Squanto for the first time. That day he negotiated a peace treaty between the Wampanoag Indians and the Pilgrims. He would live with the Pilgrims for the rest of his life, teaching them how to grow corn and where to catch fish.

CHAPTER 12

GALLOPING NORTH

BECAUSE HE WAS CHARTING the Atlantic coast of South America, Captain FitzRoy did not then continue from Tierra del Fuego on around Cape Horn and into the Pacific Ocean, but instead backtracked up the Atlantic coast to continue work on his charts. On August 3, 1833, the *Beagle* arrived at the town of Patagones at the mouth of the Río Negro, which flows from the Andes across Patagonia to the Atlantic. About 150 miles to the north was Bahía Blanca. Since the *Beagle* would be stopping at Bahía Blanca in the course of its coastal surveys, Charles decided to travel there on horseback. After meeting up with FitzRoy in Bahía Blanca, he planned to continue on land to Buenos Aires, a total of 500 miles.

Because of all the fighting between natives and Spaniards, it would have been foolish to travel overland alone, so Charles found some companions: an Englishman living in Patagones, a guide, and five gauchos. When they reached the Río Colorado, they found a division of soldiers driving a huge herd of horses across the river. Horse meat was the only food the soldiers had when

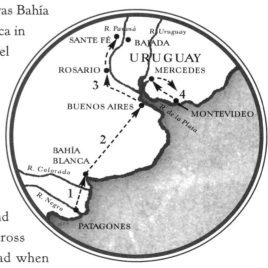

1. PATAGONES TO BAHÍA BLANCA, AUGUST 11–17, 1833

2. BAHÍA BLANCA TO BUENOS AIRES, SEPTEMBER 8–20, 1833

3. BUENOS AIRES TO SANTE FÉ, SEPTEMBER 23–OCTOBER 2, 1833

4. MONTEVIDEO TO MERCEDES, NOVEMBER 14–28, 1833

on the move. Their dinner trotted along with them.

General Rosas was camped close to the river and expressed a wish to see Darwin. Rosas was a powerful man and a legendary horseman, able to drop from a crossbar onto an unbroken horse and, without saddle or bridle, not only ride it but bring it back to the door of the corral. Darwin was curious to meet him. Later he wrote, "He is a man of extraordinary character. . . . He is said to be the owner of 74 square leagues of land, and to have about 300,000 head of cattle. His estates are admirably managed, and are far more productive of corn [in actuality, probably wheat] than any others. He first gained his celebrity by his laws for his own *estancias*, and by disciplining [training] several hundred men, so as to resist with success the attacks of the Indians."[1]

"In conversation he is enthusiastic, sensible, and very grave. . . . My interview passed away without a smile, and I obtained a passport and order for the government post-horses, and this he gave me in the most obliging and ready manner."[2]

In 1835, Rosas would become dictator of Argentina, a position he would hold until 1852.

Charles spent another few days fossil hunting at Punta Alta, where he had made his earlier finds. He was just as successful. This time he found an almost complete Megatherium (giant ground sloth) skeleton as well as some bones of what he thought was a mastodon. Unfortunately, the possible mastodon fossils crumbled in his hands and could not be preserved for shipment to England.[3]

Darwin waited for the *Beagle* in Bahía Blanca. "The place was in a constant state of excitement, from rumours

RENDERING OF A
MEGATHERIUM SKELETON

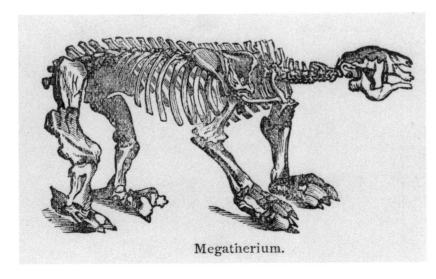

Megatherium.

of wars and victories, between the troops of Rosas and the wild Indians," he wrote later. Darwin was outraged and sickened by what he saw and heard. "Every one here is fully convinced that this is the most just war because it is against barbarians. Who would believe in this age, in a Christian civilized country, that such atrocities were committed? [Only] the children of the Indians are saved, to be sold or given away as servants."[4]

After spending about a week with Captain FitzRoy in Bahía Blanca, Darwin set off on September 8 for Buenos Aires, 400 miles away. It took him twelve days to make the trek on horseback. After a week's rest, he set off on September 27 for Santa Fe, 300 miles to the northwest. Along the way, he found a fossil tooth. He would find the skull it fitted two months later and 180 miles away!

Charles arrived in Santa Fe on October 2, 1833. Feeling sick, he spent the next two days in bed. Then he was off to Santa Fe Bajada, across the Río Paraná from Santa Fe. There he found a totally unexpected fossil: a horse tooth. When the Spanish first came to South America a few centuries earlier, there were no horses. The Spanish brought them across the Atlantic. But here was the fossil of a horse tooth many thousands of years old. Had there, then, been horses here in the distant past—horses that were extinct by the time the Spanish arrived? "Certainly it is a marvelous event in the history of animals," Charles wrote, "that a native kind [of horse] should have disappeared to be succeeded in after ages by the countless herds introduced with the Spanish colonist!"[5] Once again, Charles was puzzled and intrigued by extinct species that closely resembled species living today.

Charles returned to Buenos Aires by boat, sailing down the Río Paraná to Río de la Plata. He was almost alone on the river and felt that the splendid waterway was wasted. "We met, during our descent, very few vessels. One of the best gifts of nature seems here willfully thrown away," he wrote. "How different would have been the aspect of this river, if English colonists had by good fortune first sailed up the Plata! What noble towns would now have occupied its shores!"[6]

PAYING HIS WAY

At every major port, Charles's first stop was the local bank, where he could either draw money from his father's account or receive money orders sent from home. Charles was forever promising to spend less, but he really didn't have much choice. He paid £50 a year to Captain FitzRoy for his food and £60 a year to Syms Covington, a young crewman he had hired as his personal assistant. He also paid for all his food and lodgings on shore as well as expenses for himself and his companions on his land expeditions. In all, the trip cost Dr. Darwin £1,200—twenty times Covington's annual salary and more than twice what it would have cost had Charles stayed in England. Dr. Darwin instructed his bankers to pay every bill without question.[7]

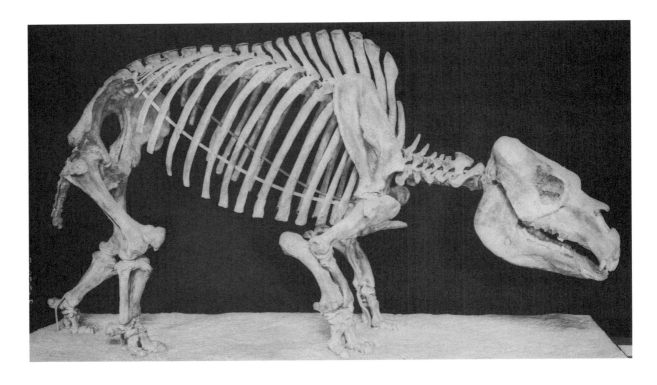

TOXODON SKELETON

Charles had intended to meet Captain FitzRoy in Buenos Aires, but when he got there, he found the city in the midst of a revolution. The ports were all closed, and the city was blockaded. Darwin found, however, that mentioning his acquaintance with General Rosas worked wonders. "Magic itself could not have altered circumstances quicker," he wrote.[8] Having entered the city, however, he found the *Beagle* had not arrived, and now he was unable to find a way to leave. At last, almost two weeks later, he "escaped" on a packet ship to Montevideo. There he found the *Beagle* and FitzRoy, who was not planning to leave for another month. So of course, Charles immediately planned another trek, this time to Mercedes, Uruguay.

CHARLES AND HIS TRAVELING COMPANIONS did not generally sleep out under the stars, though certainly that happened occasionally. In the unsettled parts of South America, they traveled from military post to military post. In the settled areas, they stayed overnight at private *estancias* (farms or ranches) along the way. At one of those *estancias* on this trip, Charles heard from his host about a giant skull at a neighboring farm. "I rode there accompanied by my host, and pur-

chased for the value of 18 pence, the head of an animal equaling in size that of the hippopotamus,"[9] Charles wrote. That animal would later be named a Toxodon—now known to be a member of an extinct group of South American mammals that lived between one and five million years ago. The people at the farmhouse told Charles that "when found, the head was quite perfect; but the boys knocked the teeth out with stones, and then set up the head as a mark to throw at."[10] The tooth that Charles had found back in October 180 miles away fit exactly into one of the tooth sockets in the skull!

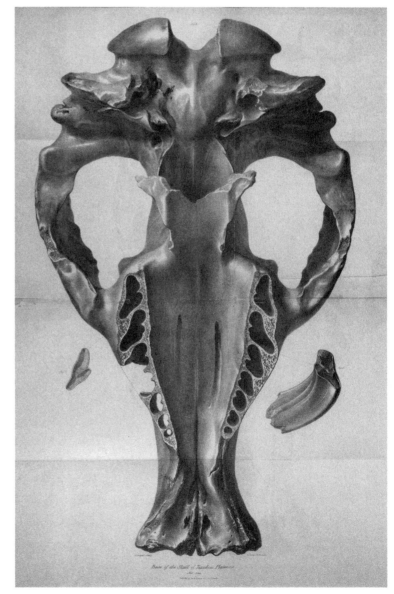

DRAWING OF A TOXODON SKULL

CHAPTER 13

EATING THE EVIDENCE

T HE *BEAGLE* SAILED from the Río de la Plata in December of 1833. On board was a new artist, Conrad Martens, who was replacing Augustus Earle, who had fallen ill. Artists were important members of scientific expeditions. They created the images that photographs provide today. The *Beagle* arrived at Port Desire (see map p.40) on December 23, 1833, just a few days shy of two years since their departure. Clearly the voyage was going to last much longer than the projected two years.

On Christmas Day, the whole crew came ashore to celebrate. Athletic contests were held, and prizes given to the winners. Darwin had shot their Christmas dinner—a guanaco, an animal from the same family as the alpaca that was large enough to feed the entire crew. A few days later, the artist Martens shot a rhea.

When he had been traveling on the Río Negro, Charles had heard the gauchos talking about a very rare bird—a smaller rhea with shorter legs than the more common rheas, and with pale blue eggs. It was said to be found in southern Patagonia, but it was seldom sighted. Darwin, of course, was eager to see one. At dinner, as he savored the meat of the bird Martens had shot, Darwin suddenly realized he was *eating* one! He dashed to the galley and was able to save the head, neck, legs, wings, many of the larger feathers, and some of the skin before the garbage could be thrown overboard. From those, John Gould, an ornithologist back in England, was able to construct a whole bird. He named it the *Rhea darwinii*, Latin for Darwin's rhea. Unfortunately a Frenchman, Alcide D'Orbigny, had been in South America six months earlier. He too had found this smaller rhea, and he'd sent a specimen back to Paris. Experts there give it another name—and the rules of scientific naming say it is the first name that counts. So, though some people still call *Avestruz petisse* "Darwin's rhea," it is more properly referred to as the "lesser rhea."

Darwin had now encountered two rhea species that ranged over the plains of southern South America in distinct areas that barely met at one point—the common rhea to the north, the lesser rhea to the south. As Charles thought about them as his voyage progressed, he realized that they posed another question of replacement. The giant armadillo indicated the replacement of an old species by a new one over *time*. As an older species became extinct and disappeared, it was replaced by a new species with different characteristics but also with some similarities. The rheas indicated replacement of one species by another in *space*. As the geographic location or territory changed, so did some characteristics of the animal. And once again, these were species that were only found in southern South America.

By this time, early in 1834, Charles had read Volume II of Charles Lyell's *Principles of Geology*, which Professor Henslow had sent to Montevideo back in November. In it, Lyell asked if there were natural processes that would modify species, making new species to replace extinct ones. Lyell answered his own question with an emphatic NO!

But so far Charles had found fossils of extinct animals, like giant armadillos, that definitely resembled living modern South American species. The ancient animals had been "replaced" by modern species.

GUANACOS

Guanacos ran wild throughout Patagonia, including Tierra del Fuego. Darwin once saw a herd of at least 500 on the banks of Río Santa Cruz. A herd was easily frightened. If, however, a man met a single animal or a small group, they would usually stand motionless, staring at him. They might then move a few yards away, turn around, and stare some more.[1]

THE *BEAGLE* BEACHED ALONG
THE SANTA CRUZ RIVER FOR
REPAIRS, DRAWN BY CONRAD
MARTENS, ONE OF THE TWO
ARTISTS ON THE VOYAGE

And now he had seen one species of rhea "replaced" by another species of rhea in a neighboring territory.

We don't know when he first began to suspect that Lyell and other scientists were wrong, but almost certainly before the *Beagle* reached home, Darwin had begun to wonder, *Why?* Why did the fossil record seem to point to species being *replaced* by other species?

CHAPTER 14

THE FUEGIAN EXPERIMENT

THE *BEAGLE* ARRIVED back in Woollya Cove, Tierra del Fuego, in March 1834 to find the wigwams deserted and the gardens untended. Jemmy showed up in his canoe—now wearing no clothes except a bit of blanket wrapped around his waist. They took him on board the *Beagle*, got him washed up and clothed in proper European manner, and set him down at the captain's table for dinner.

Jemmy remembered his English, and he still knew how to use a knife and fork. But he told them that he had no desire to return to England. His land had plenty of game and birds, he said.[1] It was his home.

Though it was hard for Englishmen to understand how anyone could turn down the advantages of civilization, they left Jemmy behind in Woollya Cove.

From Tierra del Fuego, they sailed to the Falkland Islands, which Darwin described bleakly in his journal.

> After the possession of these miserable islands had been contested by France, Spain, and England, they were left uninhabited. The government of Buenos Ayres then sold

THE *BEAGLE*, WITH
ACCOMPANYING SHIP
ADVENTURE (*SEE PAGE 65*),
AT MOUNT SARMIENTO,
MAGDALEN CHANNEL,
STRAIT OF MAGELLAN,
DRAWN BY CONRAD
MARTENS

them to a private individual, but . . . used them, as old Spain had done before, for a penal [prison] settlement. England claimed her right and seized them. The Englishman who was left in charge of the flag was consequently murdered. A British officer was next sent . . . and when we arrived, we found him in charge of a population, of which rather more than half were runaway rebels and murderers.

The theater is worthy of the scenes acted on it.[2]

But though Charles found the islands desolate, his spirits rose when he discovered that they were full of fossil brachiopods. Two-shelled sea animals, brachiopods were once among the most plentiful species on Earth.[3]

Darwin was also interested in the Falklands upland goose. These geese had no fear at all of human beings. Charles could walk right up to them. What a contrast to the geese on the mainland! Having been hunted for generations, mainland geese stayed as far away from humans as possible. Here was an example of a species changing its behavior in response to the environment.[4]

In June 1834, the *Beagle* at last passed through the Strait of Magellan, the waterway that separates Tierra del Fuego from the mainland of South America. The strait was famous for its violent seas and stories of shipwrecks. "We passed out between the East and West Furies, and a little further northward there are so many break- ers that the sea is called the Milky Way," Darwin wrote. "One sight of such a coast is enough to make a landsman dream for a week about shipwreck, peril, and death; and with this sight, we bade farewell for ever to Tierra del Fuego."[5]

They had reached the Pacific.

CHAPTER 15

EXPLOSIONS

L ATE AT NIGHT on July 23, 1834, the *Beagle* anchored in the bay of Valparaíso, Chile. The next morning, the sky was blue, the sun was shining, and "every thing appeared delightful," wrote Darwin. "All nature seemed sparkling with life."[1]

FitzRoy planned to stay in Valparaíso for some time to repair the *Beagle*, which was showing the effects of long months at sea. Happily, Charles found an old schoolmate and friend, Richard Corfield, living in the city. Corfield invited Charles to be his guest.

Valparaíso was a pretty town of whitewashed houses with red tile roofs situated at the foot of a range of steep hills. To its northeast, the Andes Mountains beckoned. Charles still considered himself first of all a geologist, and he was eager to investigate those steep slopes and mountain valleys.

On August 14, 1834, Charles set off north with Syms Covington, the young crewman who served as Darwin's personal attendant. They arrived at the Hacienda of Quintero that night. Charles had heard about great beds of shells there several yards above sea level and wanted to see them for himself. Why, he wondered, were these seashells so high above sea level?

After examining the shells the next day, he was off to the valley of

Quillota at the foot of Bell Mountain. "Whoever called 'Valparaíso' the 'Valley of Paradise' must have been thinking of Quillota," Charles wrote.[2] On the morning of the sixteenth, they set off up the mountain, which was 6,400 feet high. That evening was clear, and the view of Valparaíso, twenty-six miles away, was so sharp they could see the masts of ships in the bay.

Charles reached his destination of Santiago, Chile's capital, on August 27 and stayed for a week. He then returned to Valparaíso, taking a long route through areas he had not previously seen, arriving on September 27. But by the time he reached the home of Richard Corfield, his host in the city, he was so sick that he was in bed until the end of October.

While Charles was recuperating, Captain FitzRoy was having problems of his own. Back in Montevideo, he had purchased a schooner, a small, swift sailing vessel he hoped would make the surveying process quicker and better. The ship, renamed the *Adventure*, had been traveling with the *Beagle* ever since. FitzRoy fully expected to be reimbursed for the schooner by the Admiralty. Now he was told he would not be reimbursed; he should sell the ship immediately. The Admiralty also expressed its displeasure at the length of time it had taken the captain to survey the Atlantic coast.

FitzRoy sank into depression. His uncle had committed suicide, and then, as now, people believed strongly that depression was hereditary. The captain worried about his own mental health. He was afraid he was losing his sanity. He threatened to take the ship back to Tierra del Fuego. Then he threatened to resign.[3]

Sick and homesick as he was, when Darwin heard of the captain's resignation, he made a snap decision to leave the *Beagle* himself.

Happily for everyone, First Lieutenant John Clemens Wickham

was able to persuade FitzRoy to continue in command and not return to Tierra del Fuego but rather go forward. Though everyone's nerves were on edge, they sailed from Valparaíso, on the western coast of South America, on November 10, 1834. Their next stop would be the island of Chiloé 600 miles to the south. On the twenty-sixth, while they were surveying the Chiloean coast, they saw the volcano of Orsono spouting out volumes of smoke. A nearby volcano was spouting steam. Such sights kept Darwin busy recording his observations in his diary.

From Chiloé they turned north again to the port of Valdivia. On February 20, 1835, Charles left the ship to take a walk along the wooded shore. He had stretched out to rest when an earthquake struck. "It came on suddenly, and lasted two minutes," he wrote, "but the time appeared much longer. . . . There was no difficulty in standing upright, but the motion made me almost giddy. It was something like . . . skating over thin ice, which bends."[4]

During the quake, Captain FitzRoy and the officers were in town, where the houses shook violently but did not fall. This was not the case in Concepción, where they sailed ten days later. Concepción had been destroyed. Not a house was standing. Chairs, tables, bookcases, great bags of cotton, timber, even rooftops were scattered everywhere.

THE RUINED CATHEDRAL OF CONCEPCIÓN AFTER THE EARTHQUAKE OF FEBRUARY 20, 1835

Cows grazing on the steep hillsides had been thrown from their feet and had rolled into the sea. On a low island offshore, seventy animals had been washed off and drowned.

Charles was stunned at the destruction. What would become of England, an island nation, Charles wondered, if a natural disaster like this occurred there? The country would be bankrupt. The government would be unable to keep order. Violence, famine, and death would follow.

But geologically speaking, Charles found the earthquake fascinating. Its "most remarkable effect," Charles noted, "was the permanent elevation of the land." [5]

Captain FitzRoy, who had been educated in science at the Royal Naval College, took an active part in the *Beagle*'s scientific endeavors. He too had noticed that the land seemed to have risen. He spent the next several days taking measurements with his surveying instruments and found that the land had risen almost eight feet! A few months later he returned to measure again. The measurements were the same. The elevation was permanent.

FitzRoy sent a report to Francis Beaufort, who passed it on to Charles Lyell. Part of it was read to the Geological Society in November 1835. [6]

Based on the evidence of the raised land of Concepción, the reason for the raised banks of shells Charles had seen back in August was clear. What's more, Charles wrote, "at the same hour when the whole country around Concepción was permanently elevated, a train of volcanoes situated in the Andes, in front of Chiloé, instantaneously spouted out a dark column of smoke." [7] Over the next year, there would be uncommon volcanic activity. To the north, a volcano erupted from beneath the sea next to the island of Juan Fernández. Charles saw all these eruptions as part of the same geological event as the earthquake. "We can scarcely avoid the conclusion," he wrote, "however fearful it may be, that a vast lake of melted matter . . . is spread out beneath a mere crust of solid land." [8]

Charles believed that the whole west coast of South America had, over time and very slowly, been raised above the sea by earthquakes and volcanic action. The evidence he had witnessed supported Lyell's geologic theories conclusively.

CHAPTER 16

INTO THE
ANDES

O N MARCH 11, 1835, the *Beagle* arrived back at Valparaíso. Two days later, Charles set off overland for Santiago, where he made preparations to cross the majestic and treacherous Andes Mountains.

In that part of Chile, there were two passes across the mountains: the Uspallata and the Portillo. Charles and his companions would cross over on the Portillo pass and return on the Uspallata.

With them were ten mules, a muleteer, and a *madrina*. The *madrina* (meaning godmother) was an old mule with a bell around her neck. Wherever she went, the other mules would follow. Each mule knew the sound of its own *madrina*'s bell. So if the mules were grazing with other pack animals, all the muleteer had to do was lead his *madrina* a little way off and her tinkling bell would summon the others.

Six of the mules were for riding and four for carrying supplies— about 300 pounds per mule. They took a lot of food in case they got snowed in on the high mountain passes. Darwin's group was crossing the Portillo pass late in the season, so snow was a real threat.

As Charles and his companions set out up the valley, the vegetation thinned. Birds and animals too seemed to disappear. But the geology was striking. The lowest elevations were a dull red or purple claystone porphyry (a kind of igneous rock). Above that was a layer of gypsum. In places, the gypsum layer was 2,000 feet thick. This was gradually replaced by a layer of red sandstone and black clay slate. Embedded in the black slate were numerous shells and deposits from the sea. Shells, once at the bottom of the sea, had been lifted nearly 14,000 feet above sea level! Darwin could scarcely contain his excitement. Everywhere he looked, the story of ancient upheavals was written in the rocks.

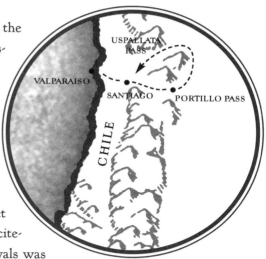

DARWIN'S PASSAGE OVER THE ANDES

As the group got higher, the atmosphere thinned. There was less oxygen in the air, and the mules would halt every fifty yards to catch their breath for a few seconds. The people were short of breath, too. The Chileans called this condition *puna* and pointed out graves along the way of people who had died of it. Charles was skeptical. "The only sensation I felt was a slight tightness over the head and chest," he wrote, and "upon finding fossil shells on the highest ridge, I entirely forgot the puna in my delight." The Chileans "all recommend onions for the puna. . . . For my part, I found nothing so good as the fossil shells!"[1]

At the top of the mountains, the atmosphere was so clear and thin that the moon and stars shone with exceptional brilliance. The effect was magical.[2]

The descent down the eastern side of the mountains was steeper than on the Pacific side. Beneath them was a band of clouds, which they soon entered. The clouds surrounded the small party for an entire day. The plants and animals on the eastern side of the Andes were the same as those Charles had seen on the Atlantic coast of Patagonia. On the western, Pacific side of the Andes, the plants were very different. Charles thought this odd, since the climate and soil on both sides were nearly identical.[3]

On March 29, they set out on their return to Chile by the Uspallata pass. The next day Charles observed dozens of snow-white columns projecting from a bare slope about 7,000 feet above sea level. They were petrified trees. But they had not grown at this elevation. And certainly not at the strange angle at which they were now standing. Charles felt sure the ghostly trees had grown in volcanic soil. That soil would have come from an oceanic eruption when Patagonia was being raised from the sea. In his mind's eye, Charles could picture a cluster of trees waving their branches "on the shores of the Atlantic, back when that ocean (now driven back 700 miles) approached the base of the Andes."[4] Just as the land in Concepción had risen after the earthquake, the land these trees had originally grown in had been pushed up, bit by bit—up 7,000 feet to form majestic mountains!

Charles concluded that the eastern range of the Andes had been made *after* the western range. It was a radical thought, but he was sure he was correct. It seemed that during the voyage of the *Beagle* and his overland treks in South America, the seeds of new and radical thoughts were constantly being planted in the mind of Charles Darwin.

CHAPTER 17

THE GALAPAGOS

IN SEPTEMBER 1835, the *Beagle* left South America and headed home across the Pacific Ocean. Their first stop along the way was the Galapagos Islands.

The Galapagos are an archipelago, a cluster of islands, in the Pacific Ocean about 600 hundred miles off the coast of Ecuador. There are thirteen major islands, eight smaller islands, and forty islets scattered over an area of about 27,900 square miles (45,000 square kilometers).

"Ecuador" means "equator," and the Galapagos lie smack on top of the equator, the imaginary belt around the middle of the Earth. Considering this, Charles noted, the temperatures were not overly hot. He thought this was probably due to the low temperature of the surrounding sea. In fact, the currents around the Galapagos are cold enough that a species of small penguin lives there.

Charles saw that the islands were volcanic—and he guessed that they were not especially old geologically. We now know that the oldest of the islands are only a few million years old, fairly young in geologic time. The Galapagos are slowly moving southeastward over a "hot spot" in the Pacific floor, with new volcanic islands form-

THE GALAPAGOS ISLANDS

ABINGDON

TOWER

BINDLOE

EQUATOR

JAMES

BALTRA

INDEFATIGABLE

NARBOROUGH

DUNCAN

BARRINGTON CHATHAM

ALBEMARLE

CHARLES HOOD

THE GALAPAGOS PENGUIN

The Galapagos penguin is one of the smallest penguins, standing only 16-18 inches (40-45 cm) tall and weighing only five pounds (2 to 2.5 kg). While other penguins have to cope with temperatures as low as -75° F (-60° C), the Galapagos penguin must cope with the heat. Temperatures in the archipelago can rise to over 100° F (38° C). To keep cool, the small penguins hunt and swim in the cold water. When on land they hold their flippers out to help heat escape their bodies and to shade their feet to prevent sunburn. This unique species lives only in the Galapagos.

ing periodically in the northern part of the archipelago.

Most of the islands are dry and rocky with grass-filled fields. There are a number of mountains, and the land is pocked with many craters. Charles guessed there must be at least 2,000 craters in all the islands. Here and there are areas of woodlands as well. All these conditions make for a variety of habitats.

Today the Galapagos Islands are one of the few places on Earth where wildlife is so tame that visitors can walk right up to it. There are several species of boobies—large birds that dive for fish—that nest right along the pathways humans use. The boobies don't move when someone approaches. Even the Galapagos hawk lets people get very close.

Galapagos birds haven't learned to fear people for the simple reason that they were never bothered by humans. The islands were a Spanish colony when the *Beagle* arrived, but people hadn't been living there long. Sailors had brought goats to the islands. The goats bred, providing a reliable source of food for ships passing by. People—both settlers and sailors—had been killing Galapagos tortoises for their meat for years, but overall, the wildlife was never seriously threatened by hunters or disturbed by farmers. When Charles arrived, the native birds held no fear.

In 1835, the Galapagos were already known for the great variety of animals that lived nowhere else on Earth. Lyell had written about them in the second volume of *Principles of Geology.* Had they immigrated from other areas? he wondered.[1] Lyell was certain there were no large animals on the Galapagos. The islands were simply too far from land for large animals to have migrated there.[2]

What grabbed Charles's attention was how the animals varied from island to island. The tortoises, for example. The governor of the Galapagos told him that people living there could tell at a glance which island a tortoise had come from by the appearance of its shell. Charles didn't pay much attention to the story at first, though he was interested

TED LEWIN

GALAPAGOS TORTOISES

The differences between Galapagos tortoises can be quite dramatic. For example, dome-shelled tortoises have shells that do not allow them to raise their heads very high. These tortoises graze along the ground. But saddle-backed tortoises have shells that are higher at the front, allowing them to graze on the taller vegetation in their habitat.

Galapagos tortoises can live more than 150 years and grow to 600 pounds. They are very peaceful creatures and easy to catch. Sailors in Darwin's time would catch them and stow them live in the ship's cargo hold for up to a year. They then killed and ate the fresh meat as they needed it. One tortoise could provide 200 pounds of meat. There were once more than 200,000 tortoises on the Galapagos Islands, but due in part to this practice, today there are only around 10,000.

in the tortoises. Some, he was told, were so large it took six or eight men to lift them from the ground. He was fascinated to see the Chatham Island tortoises make their way to drinking water on well-worn paths. "Near the springs," he wrote, "it was a curious spectacle to behold many of these great monsters; one set eagerly traveling onwards with outstretched necks, and another set returning, after having drunk their fill."[3]   Charles frequently got on their backs and rode them, though he had a hard time keeping his balance.[4] But for once he didn't collect many specimens. Though he and the crew dined on tortoise regularly (one tortoise could feed the entire crew), they simply threw the shells into the sea.

MARINE IGUANA

NILES ELDREDGE

GALAPAGOS IGUANAS

The Galapagos are home to two species of iguana. The marine iguana feeds in the ocean off algae and seaweed. It is the only iguana in the world that swims and feeds in the ocean. Charles experimented with one by tossing it into the water over and over—it always returned to land and let him do it again. The land iguana lives on land and eats prickly pear cactus. It can go for a full year without any water other than what is in the cactus.

Both iguanas appeared peculiarly adapted to life in the Galapagos Islands, and in fact they can be found nowhere else on Earth.

It was only after he got home that Charles read that the tortoises were different species and *native* to each island, not migrants from somewhere else. Then he began to take the story of their variations more seriously. Nor did Charles see the importance of the little black, brown, and greenish birds today known as "Darwin's finches." He saw the birds, all right. But he mistakenly thought they belonged to different groups. At least in this case, he did collect specimens, though unusually for Darwin, he did not keep good notes on which island each bird came from. When he brought them home, the ornithologist John Gould (the same person who had pieced together "Darwin's rhea") told him there were thirteen distinct species, and they were all

LAND IGUANA

TED LEWIN

DAISY TREES

On the Galapagos Islands, plants resembling daisies grew to the size of trees—over 32 feet (10 m) tall! Darwin found six species of these trees, which live only in the Galapagos. But what was even more remarkable was that each species was found on only *one* island.

SOME OF THE GALAPAGOS ISLANDS, *(FROM TOP TO BOTTOM)*: CHARLES ISLAND, CHATHAM ISLAND, "WATERY PLACE," AND ALBEMARLE ISLAND

closely related members of a single group of finches.

But Charles did *not* miss the mockingbirds. Mockingbirds, like sloths and armadillos, occur only in the New World—North and South America. He found one type of mockingbird on Charles Island, another on Albemarle Island, and a third on James and Chatham Islands. The Charles Island mockingbird lived nowhere else. The same was true for the Albemarle mockingbird. And the same again with the James and Chatham mockingbirds. "I examined many specimens in the different islands," Charles wrote, "and in each the respective kind was *alone* present."[5]

Charles was not sure whether the different mockingbirds were separate species or different varieties of a single species. But either way, why were there different looking mockingbirds on these islands? Why did one kind of mockingbird "replace" another on the next island? Here was the rhea question again. Why did whole populations of animals change in their characteristics from one location to another?

MOCKINGBIRDS, HOOD ISLAND

TED LEWIN

CHAPTER 18

SAILING HOME

THE *BEAGLE* STAYED in the Galapagos from September 15 to October 20, 1835, just a little more than a month. As the ship slowly crossed the Pacific, stopping at Tahiti, New Zealand, and Australia, Charles kept up his collecting and observing. They spent Christmas in New Zealand. "In a few more days, the fourth year of our

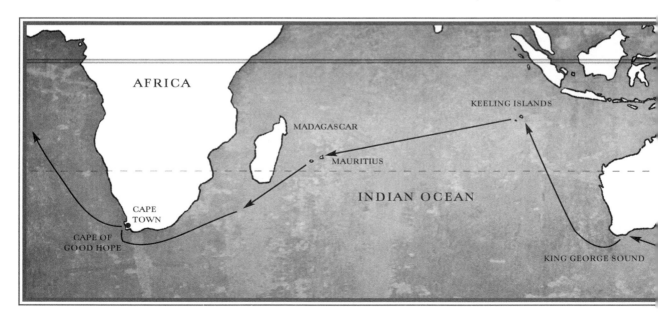

AFRICA

KEELING ISLANDS

MADAGASCAR

MAURITIUS

INDIAN OCEAN

CAPE
TOWN

CAPE OF
GOOD HOPE

KING GEORGE SOUND

absence from England will be completed," Charles wrote on Christmas Day. "The next [Christmas], I trust in providence, will be in England."[1]

Probably the most important event for Darwin on their trip home came during a brief stopover in Cape Town, South Africa, in May 1836. While there, Charles went to visit Sir John Herschel, the famous English astronomer whose book *Introduction to the Study of Natural Philosophy*, had inspired Charles back at Cambridge. Herschel was in Cape Town to make astronomical observations of the sky in the southern hemisphere.

Herschel also knew Charles Lyell personally. Lyell's ideas about the gradual formation of the Earth had interested him, and he had written to Lyell wondering when a naturalist would appear who would explain what Herschel called the "mystery of mysteries," the question of how and why new species arose to replace ones that had gone extinct. No one knows for sure what Darwin and Sir John talked about. No doubt Lyell and geology came up, but it's possible they discussed the mystery as well.

In any case, on the way home, Charles began to write up his notes. He'd been writing about birds, but when he came to the mockingbird,

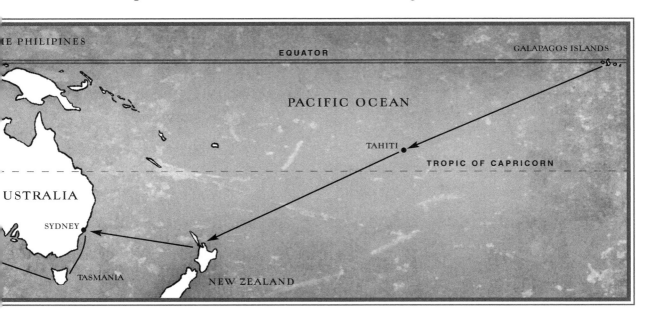

he suddenly recalled what the governor of the Galapagos had told him about different tortoises on different islands.

In *Principles of Geology*, Lyell had been adamant that transmutation—the changing of one animal into another—could not exist. If there were two rheas in South America, or three mockingbirds on four islands in the Galapagos, or who knew how many tortoises, then those rheas, mockingbirds, and tortoises had *always* been there with the same characteristics they had today. One species could *not* have transformed into another. All species were stable. That is, all species stayed the same. To Lyell, the order of nature and the

JOHN HERSCHEL

A mathematician, astronomer, and photographic inventor, John Herschel was one of the most famous scientists of his day. In addition to his many astronomical achievements (among other things, he mapped and named seven of Saturn's moons and four of Uranus's), he experimented with color photography, and indeed coined the word *photography*. Herschel Island in the Arctic Ocean and J. Herschel crater on the moon are named after him.

meaning of humankind depended on this.

Charles was not inclined to disagree with the celebrated scientist. But Lyell had been mistaken in his belief that there were no large animals on the Galapagos. Not only were there the giant tortoises, there were giant iguanas as well. Charles remembered how the people of the islands could tell at once from which island a tortoise had come. He recalled how close the islands had been to one another. Here were animals very similar but with some unmistakable differences inhabiting places only very slightly different from one another. And then there were all the different mockingbirds.

At first Darwin thought they were all varieties of the same species. "When I see these islands in sight of each other . . . tenanted by these birds, but slightly differing in structure & filling the same place in Nature, I must suspect they are only varieties," he wrote in his Ornithological Notes. Perhaps the different varieties might be the *beginning* of new species, he speculated. But what if the varieties grew so different that they actually *became* new species? "If there is the slightest foundation for these remarks," he continued, "such facts would undermine the stability of Species."[2]

There it was! Charles was beginning to think that species were *not* stable, not forever fixed and unchanging. He saw the variation in mockingbirds and tortoises on the different Galapagos islands as a clue that new species can originate from old ones.

Charles knew that extinct species were replaced by new ones of the same basic group. He had seen the giant armadillo fossils and he had seen the living armadillos. He had also seen different forms of rheas, mockingbirds, and tortoises. This was evidence that living species of one region can be replaced by other living species in another region. He was beginning to suspect that some new species arose naturally from old species.

He wasn't yet ready to push his evidence to its logical conclusion that *all* species arose from old species, but he was on his way.

CHAPTER 19

HOME AT LAST

AFTER NEARLY FIVE YEARS, Darwin was eager to get home. So he was understandably dismayed when, at the last minute, Captain FitzRoy made an unexpected detour back across the Atlantic to Brazil to take additional measurements. But at last, on October 2, 1836, the *Beagle* returned to England. By then, Darwin's ideas about his future had changed. Though he had often written his sisters about his future as a clergyman, by the end of the voyage, he was no longer enthusiastic about a career as a pastor. Instead, he wanted to become a man of science like Lyell—not tied to the church, but independent.[1]

Happily, he already had a reputation as a scientist. In great part, this was thanks to Professor Henslow. Henslow had already gotten some of Darwin's fossils into the right hands. He also made sure that Darwin's views were heard in the scientific and academic community. In November 1835, he had read parts of Darwin's letters to the Cambridge Philosophical Society. He had persuaded Professor Sedgwick to read the papers at a meeting of the Geological Society, where Charles Lyell had heard them. Lyell was eager to meet this young man.[2]

Charles now picked up where Henslow had left off. The first order

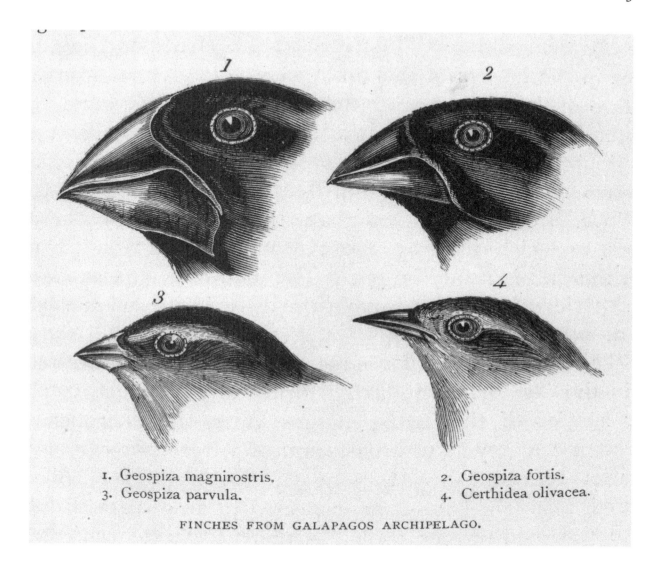

1. Geospiza magnirostris.
2. Geospiza fortis.
3. Geospiza parvula.
4. Certhidea olivacea.

FINCHES FROM GALAPAGOS ARCHIPELAGO.

DARWIN'S FINCHES

Back in London, Charles Darwin was surprised to learn from ornithologist John Gould that a group of bird specimens he had brought back from the Galapagos were all finches. They looked so different from one another that Charles had assumed they were all different birds. Unfortunately, he hadn't kept track of where he had collected each finch! Here Captain FitzRoy and other crewmembers came to the rescue. They had also collected finch specimens and, happily, had taken better notes of where they'd found them.

VOYAGE OF THE *BEAGLE*

In 1839, Darwin's *Journal and Remarks, 1832–1836* was published with three other volumes by Captain FitzRoy in a set titled *Narrative of the Surveying Voyages of His Majesty's Ships Adventure and Beagle.* Unlike FitzRoy's volumes, Darwin's volume was what we might today call a good read, so not surprisingly, it was more popular than the other volumes. The publisher therefore decided to reissue it on its own under the title *Journal of researches into the geology and natural history of the various countries visited by H.M.S. Beagle.* He did this without mentioning it to Darwin and without paying him a cent, as the publishing contract was with Captain FitzRoy, not with Charles Darwin. Charles found another publisher for the next edition. Known today as *Voyage of the Beagle,* it is still available.

of business was to get all his specimens into the hands of experts to be studied. He had sent crates of them back from South America, and he brought more home on board—animal and bird remains, pickled fish, dried insects and plants, and fossils. Henslow would study the plants. Professor Richard Owen of the Royal College of Surgeons would study the fossil mammals. Ornithologist John Gould at the Regent's Park Zoo would study the birds.

Charles joined the Geological Society. He was also elected to the Athenaeum Club, a gentleman's club of great fame whose membership included the novelist Charles Dickens.[3] At Lyell's request, Darwin prepared a paper on his observations of the elevation of the coast of Chile.[4] And he began work on his first book—an account of his adventures on the *Beagle.* Captain FitzRoy had invited him to write the natural history section of his four-volume account of the voyage. Darwin's *Journal and Remarks, 1832–1836* would be Volume III.

On March 7, 1837, Charles moved into his brother Ras's house on Great Marlborough Street in London. He would stay there for the next two years, until he married in January 1839. During that time he would read several papers before the Geological Society, complete his work on *Journal and Remarks,* and begin a second book, *Geological Observations.* "During these two years I also went a little into society," Charles wrote in his autobiography. "I saw a great deal of Lyell," he continued, and "as I was not able to work all day at science I read a good deal."[5]

About this time Darwin began work on what would be his most famous book and greatest contribution to scientific thought. Many years later, he wrote in his autobiography, "In July [1837], I opened my first note-book for facts in relation to the *Origin of Species,* about which I had long reflected, and never ceased working on for the next twenty years."[6]

By then, Professor Owen, who had been studying Darwin's fossils, had confirmed that the extinct glyptodonts were indeed forms of giant armadillos. And Darwin had seen the different rheas for himself.

This was enough to convince Charles that life had evolved, but how? Why? Darwin began looking for more clues to evolution. He found one right away when he thought about the classification of animals and plants.

In Darwin's time, biologists had been using the system of classification devised by the Swedish botanist Carolus Linnaeus in 1758 for a hundred years. Linnaeus grouped closely similar species into what he called a "genus." Our own species is called *Homo sapiens* (meaning Wise man). *Sapiens* is the name of our species. *Homo* is the name of our genus. Other members of our genus are now all extinct: *Homo neanderthalensis* (Neanderthal man), *Homo erectus* (upright man), *Homo ergaster* (working man), *Homo habilis* (handy man), and the recently discovered *Homo floresiensis* (Floresian man—named for the island of

RICHARD OWEN

Flores in Indonesia where its bones were found). All members of the genus *Homo* are part of the Hominidae family.

Every species—humans, squirrels, pine trees—is classified with a group of other species it most resembles. These groups of species are in turn similar to other groups of species. Hominids, our family, also contains gorillas, chimpanzees, and orangutans, which are all part of the order called primates. We share over 98 percent of our genes with chimpanzees, and our skeletons are very similar. The next closest relatives to humans and apes are the monkeys of Africa and Asia, which are primates, but not hominids. Other groups of species are more distantly related.

Darwin realized that this progressive natural grouping of animals and plants is precisely what you would expect if evolution had occurred—if newer species developed out of older ones. The rheas of South America would be related to extinct fossil rheas first, but then also to the African ostrich and the Australian emu. This would mean that rheas did not evolve *from* ostriches or emus, but rather that ostriches, emus, and rheas all evolved from something else, a common ancestor many thousands of years in the past. Likewise, the close similarity of human, ape, and monkey skeletons is what you would expect if evolution occurred, if species changed or "evolved" with the passage of time and change of location. Humans would not have evolved from apes or monkeys but would share a common ancestor with them.

Charles also knew that in the early stages, embryos of dogs, chickens, rats, lizards, and people are very similar—differences between species appear gradually as the embryo develops. That close resemblance in the early stages of embryos, Charles said, is what you would expect if all these species of vertebrate animals (animals with

LIFE IN THE 1830s

In 1830, William IV became King of England, Andrew Jackson was president of the United States, and Ecuador became an independent nation. In England, ladies' hats were extremely large and adorned with ribbons and flowers, and stiff collars were the fashion for men. In 1831, when Darwin set sail, chloroform was invented and London Bridge opened to traffic. The population of England was then 13.9 million and of the United States 12.8 million, more than 2.3 million of whom were black. Horse-drawn trolleys first appeared on the streets of New York in 1832, and England abolished slavery in 1833. Hans Christian Andersen published his first children's stories in 1835. The following year, Davy Crockett was killed at the Alamo and the first cricket match was played. William IV died in 1837 and Victoria became Queen of England. She would reign until 1901. In 1838, as steamships began to cross the Atlantic, Frederick Douglass escaped from slavery, Charles Dickens's novel Oliver Twist was a bestseller, and England went to war with the Afghans. The First Anglo-Afghan War would last until 1842. In 1839, Cinque led the mutiny aboard the Amistad, and England went to war with China in the First Opium War. This war would also end in 1842.

backbones) came from a common ancestral species long ago.

Charles also knew that selection was the key to man's success in breeding better animals and plants. Any dairy farmer knew that if you bred only your best milkers, you would get better milkers. But how could this selection work in nature? Cows couldn't decide for themselves to create better milkers.

And then, in the autumn of 1838, Charles happened to read an old book, *Essay on the Principle of Population*, by Thomas Malthus, first published in 1798. Malthus was writing about human population and the miseries suffered by the poor when famine strikes. *Food* affected the size of the population. In times of plenty, the population increased. In hard times, more people died.

Charles also realized that many more offspring—whether they are humans or rheas or finches—are born each generation than can survive and reproduce. If every elephant born survived and had babies, the world would soon be overrun with elephants. Something had to be controlling the number of individuals in each species—and for the most part, that "something" was the food supply.

Charles also knew that individual organisms vary, even within the same species. Except for identical twins, no two are exactly alike. And he knew that organisms resemble their parents. Because more offspring were born each generation than could possibly survive and reproduce, Charles concluded that for the most part, only those organisms that were best able to find food and meet their other basic needs would survive and reproduce. Because organisms tend to resemble their parents, the traits that enabled the parents to survive—such as longer, stronger legs to help them run faster, or keener eyesight, or thicker hair, or better camouflage—would be passed on to the next generation. If the environment didn't change, those organisms with those traits would continue to survive. The successful traits would become even more pronounced. If the environment did change, however, other traits might then become more important for making a living.

Charles called this idea "natural selection." Just as farmers could breed sheep, cattle, and plants to improve their wool, increase the amount of milk they gave, or make different sorts of apples, a similar process in nature selected individuals with certain traits to survive and reproduce based on how well those traits helped the creature deal with its environment.

But he hesitated to publish his conclusions. It was one thing to write a paper on the geology of the Andes or to publish a book about his adventures on the *Beagle*. It was quite another to go against all the scientific, social, and religious wisdom of the ages. Nearly everyone in England believed that species were created separately by God and were permanent and unchanging, the same today as they were when God had made them. Charles was simply afraid to be seen as a man who would use science and logic to deny the literal truth of stories in the Bible.

Nevertheless, as Charles Darwin read and studied and sifted through his notes and memories of the *Beagle* voyage, his understanding of the evolution of life became clearer and clearer. Here at last was the answer to his great question of: Why?

CHAPTER 20

FAMILY LIFE
AND HUMAN
EVOLUTION

B Y 1838, CHARLES HAD BEGUN to think of marriage. But he
worried that a wife and family might interfere with his scientific
career, forcing him into a social life he didn't want, and restrict-
ing his time at study and with fellow scientists. Being a man of science
and logic, he drew up a list of the pros and cons of married life. In the
end, he decided that a settled life with wife and children and a companion to grow old with was far more attractive than the freedom of bach-
elorhood. He decided to propose to his first cousin, Emma Wedgwood.
She was the daughter of his Uncle Jos, Darwin's mother's brother, who
had convinced Dr. Darwin that Charles should sail on the *Beagle*.

On Sunday, November 11, 1838, Charles proposed to Emma at the
Wedgwood family home, Maer Hall. Emma had known Charles since
childhood—he was the cousin who hunted with her father and brothers;
she was the charming, messy, adored baby of the Wedgwood family. But
Charles had never expressed any amorous feelings toward her, and she

EMMA WEDGWOOD DARWIN IN 1840

CHARLES DARWIN IN 1840

THE PROS AND CONS
OF MARRIAGE

As Charles saw it, the arguments for not marrying included avoiding "the expense and anxiety of children" and the amount of his time a wife might take up. "How should I manage all my business if I were obliged to go every day walking with my wife," he wrote. "I never should know French, or see the Continent, or go to America, or go up in a Balloon."

His arguments *for* marriage included some of the same things: "Children (if it please God)" and a wife who would be a "constant companion (and friend in old age)." [1]

was certainly not expecting a proposal of marriage from him. Charles, in turn, was taken by surprise when Emma accepted him. Emma was "bewildered." Charles had a headache. Uncle Jos was delighted.[2]

The rest of the family shared Uncle Jos's opinion: Charles and Emma would make an excellent match. Their prediction turned out to be true.

"I think you will humanize me, & soon teach me there is greater happiness, than building theories, & accumulating facts in silence and solitude," Charles wrote to Emma in January 1839. "My own dearest Emma, I earnestly pray, you may never regret the great, & I will add very good, deed, you are to perform on the Tuesday [the day of their wedding]: my own dear future wife, God bless you."[3]

Once Emma had gotten used to the notion, she was equally enthusiastic. "He is the most open, transparent man I ever saw," she wrote to her aunt, "and every word expresses his real thoughts. He is particularly affectionate and very nice to his father and sisters, and perfectly sweet tempered, and possesses some minor qualities that add particularly to one's happiness, such as not being fastidious, and being humane to animals."[4]

Charles and Emma were married on January 29, 1839, two weeks before Charles's thirtieth birthday. They moved into a rented house on Upper Gower Street in London. It was a colorful place with bright blue walls, yellow curtains, and red furniture—they called it "Macaw Cottage."

Their life in London was full of visiting and receiving friends and family, and attending concerts and other events.[5] One of their first purchases was a piano, and Emma often played for Charles in the evenings.[6] She was a fine pianist and had taken lessons from the famous composer and pianist Frédéric Chopin.[7]

The Darwins' first child, William Erasmus, was born in December of that same year. A few days before the birth, Charles, concerned and nervous, got sick with headaches and nausea. Similar illnesses would plague him for the rest of his life, often occurring during stressful times. But he was thrilled with the new baby and started charting William's development immediately. He wrote down all the details of William's yawns, hiccups, sneezes, and cries. He recorded the baby's first smile

FAMILY MARRIAGES

Marriages between first cousins were common in the upper classes of the nineteenth century. Young men didn't have to look far for a bride, plus such marriages kept family fortunes in the family. Charles Darwin's maternal grandmother had married a first cousin, and his sister Caroline had married her cousin Josiah, Emma's brother.

JENNY THE ORANGUTAN, ONE
OF TWO "JENNYS" WHO WERE
THE FIRST ORANGUTANS TO
COME TO THE REGENT'S PARK
ZOO IN LONDON

and his reaction on first seeing himself in a mirror. He even studied the wrinkles around his eyes when he was angry. He experimented with William by making noises close to him and observing his reactions.[8]

Two years earlier, in 1837, the Regent's Park Zoo had gotten its first orangutan, which they named Jenny. Charles was fascinated with her. As a member of the Zoological Society, he was allowed into her cage. He had watched Jenny closely and taken notes. When he gave her a mirror, she was fascinated with her own reflection. When he played a harmonica, then handed it to Jenny, she imitated him and raised it to her mouth. When she was angry, she kicked and cried like a naughty child, and when she'd been naughty, she hid beneath a blanket.

Now Charles was curious to compare Jenny with William. It was clear to him that very young human children and very young orangutans were quite similar. The differences between the species increased as the youngsters got older, but Charles had no problem seeing the connections between apes and people. Though he took careful notes and was excited by his observations, he continued to keep his thoughts to himself. He was well aware that any suggestion that humans and apes were related, even distantly, would be met with outrage.

Charles and Emma's next child, a daughter they named Anne Elizabeth, was born in March 1841. Charles became sick again.[9] But he was as enchanted with his daughter as he had been with his son. No two children could be so wonderful, so fascinating as these!

Of course, Charles studied Annie too. He noted her first smile when she was forty-six days old, and later how she wrinkled her nose when she smiled. He paid particular attention to the similarities between Annie and her brother. Annie seemed much more patient than Willy, less likely to get frustrated at small things.[10] She was also very precise. When she was only fourteen months old, she held pens and pencils just like an adult would hold them. Willy, on the other hand, couldn't hold them well at all, even though he was older.[11]

Macaw Cottage was a happy home for the Darwins, but the city in which they lived was not without its problems. London at that time was a city of two million people. A wealthy metropolis filled with clubs, concert halls, scientific associations, publishers, and institutions of higher learning, it was also the seat of the English government. But the streets were snarled with carriage traffic and smeared with horse droppings. The air was thick with coal dust, which blackened buildings and laundry alike. There was no place for the Darwin children to play. And with Charles and Emma, two children, a nurse, and various household servants, Macaw Cottage was beginning to get crowded. Charles had fond memories of his boyhood rambles in woods and meadows. The Darwins began to look for a house in the quieter countryside. They found the perfect place—a large white house with

---

LIFE IN THE 1840s

In the 1840s, Connecticut, Massachusetts, and Pennsylvania all passed laws limiting the hours a day children could work in textile factories. By 1841, the population had grown to 18.5 million in England and 17 million in the United States. That same year, a Scottish surgeon, James Braid, discovered hypnosis, university degrees were granted to women in the United States for the first time, and the U.S. Supreme Court ruled in favor of the Amistad Africans. Ether was first used for surgery in 1842, and the first appendectomy was performed in 1848. Sojourner Truth began her abolitionist work in 1843. Popular novels of the decade included The Old Curiosity Shop (1841) and A Christmas Carol (1843) by Charles Dickens, Jane Eyre (1847) by Charlotte Brontë, and Wuthering Heights (1847) by her sister Emily. The YMCA was founded, and Morse's telegraph was used for the first time (between Baltimore and Washington) in 1844. The California Gold Rush began in 1848. Inventions of the decade included safety matches and ladies' bloomers.

extensive gardens just outside the tiny village of Down (renamed Downe in the 1850s)[12] about sixteen miles southeast of London. They moved to "Down House" in 1842.

In June of that same year, Charles Darwin wrote out a short summary of his species theory for the first time. It was only thirty-five pages long. He knew he still needed to gather much more data in order to convince anyone he was right. He also knew his ideas would be seen by many as an attack on religion. The time, he felt, was not right to make his thoughts public.

Charles threw himself into improving their new home. He planted flowers and fruit trees, purchased cows and a horse and cart, supervised construction to enlarge the house, organized his study, and got a kitchen garden under way. He also became active in local politics and got to know the neighbors.[13]

In September 1842, Emma gave birth to their third child, Mary Eleanor. Sadly she died before she was three weeks old. A fourth child, Henrietta, whom they called Etty, came a year later, in September 1843.

DURING THE SUMMER OF 1844, two years after moving into Down House, Charles expanded his 35-page summary on species theory to 230 pages. But he was still afraid to publish and face the wrath of scientists and religious leaders who would be offended by his ideas. Instead, he wrote a letter to Emma with detailed instructions to publish his writings after his death.[14]

He also wrote to his new friend, the

CHARLES WITH WILLIAM DARWIN, THE DARWINS' FIRST CHILD

botanist Joseph Hooker, whom he had met in 1843 after Hooker returned from a five-year Antarctic expedition. A respected expert on plant life, Joseph Hooker took on the work of describing and identifying the plants Darwin had collected on the *Beagle*. The two quickly became close and trusted friends, and would remain so for the rest of their lives.

"I have been now ever since my return engaged in a very presumptuous work," Darwin wrote to Hooker. "At last gleams of light have come, & I am almost convinced (quite contrary to the opinion I started with) that species are not (it is like confessing a murder) immutable [unchangeable]. . . . I think I have found out (here's presumption!) the simple way by which species become adapted to various ends."[15]

Much to his surprise and delight, Hooker was willing to discuss Darwin's theory with him. Perhaps some in the scientific community would not automatically dismiss his ideas after all.

JOSEPH HOOKER

IN NOVEMBER 1844, Charles read a new book titled *Vestiges of the Natural History of Creation.* The anonymous author (now known to be Robert Chambers from Edinburgh, Scotland) wrote about the changes in the Earth from the very beginning of time and the changes in life on Earth. Darwin was stunned. Though Chambers did not explain the How or Why of his theories and lacked any firsthand evidence, his general *evolutionary* thesis was the same as Darwin's own—though, to Darwin's relief, Chambers had not written about natural selection.

Vestiges was an immediate success. It was reprinted three times in its first year, published in the United States in 1845, and translated into German in 1851. Everyone was reading it, from Alfred, Lord Tennyson to Ralph Waldo Emerson to Florence Nightingale to Abraham Lincoln. The reviews, whether pro or con, were impassioned.

A SOURCE OF ANXIETY

While Emma was a devout Christian, Charles was not. By the time of their engagement, he was no longer certain he believed in God at all. That she might not spend eternity with her husband would be a source of sorrow for Emma all her life. Yet she would never fail in her love for Charles or her support for his life's work.

In spite of the commercial success of the book, the scientific community by and large rejected *Vestiges*. Professor Sedgwick, in particular, raged against it. Not only was the book shallow, he maintained, it was written by a hack with no scientific knowledge, and on top of everything, it denied the word of God. Darwin was shocked by Sedgwick's venomous attack.[16] Though Charles's evidence *was* firsthand and his scientific reputation was established, would his own book about evolution be similarly greeted? After all, he was not a botanist or biologist either.

CHAPTER 21

LIFE AT
DOWN HOUSE

BY JANUARY 1849, Charles and Emma had six children: William, born in 1839 and now nine, Anne (born 1841), Henrietta (Etty, born 1843), George (born 1845), Elizabeth (Betty, born 1847), and Francis (born 1848). Three more children were yet to come: Leonard in 1850, Horace in 1851, and Charles in 1856. One child, Mary Eleanor, had been born in 1842 but lived for only three weeks.

With six children all under ten years old, Down House was a lively place. When Emma and Charles had married, they had discussed what to do about their expensive furniture: Should they keep the children off it? Or should they let them play on it as they wished? They had decided not to worry about the furniture; the children would be welcome to play on it. Sometimes they pushed all the drawing room furniture to one side of the room. Then Emma would play "the galloping tune" on the piano and the children would gallop around the room.[1]

When they were little, Charles often played with the children. He liked to tickle his daughters' knees, chanting, "If you be a fair lady as I do hope you be, then you will not laugh at the tickling of your knee." The children liked to pat their father's hairy chest while he growled at them like a bear.[2] A game that Annie and Etty especially loved when they were small they called "Taglioni." The Taglionis were a famous ballet family, and the game consisted of dancing on their daddy's knees.[3]

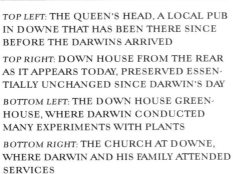

TOP LEFT: THE QUEEN'S HEAD, A LOCAL PUB IN DOWNE THAT HAS BEEN THERE SINCE BEFORE THE DARWINS ARRIVED

TOP RIGHT: DOWN HOUSE FROM THE REAR AS IT APPEARS TODAY, PRESERVED ESSENTIALLY UNCHANGED SINCE DARWIN'S DAY

BOTTOM LEFT: THE DOWN HOUSE GREENHOUSE, WHERE DARWIN CONDUCTED MANY EXPERIMENTS WITH PLANTS

BOTTOM RIGHT: THE CHURCH AT DOWNE, WHERE DARWIN AND HIS FAMILY ATTENDED SERVICES

The boys played with Charles's bola and boomerang, brought back from South America and Australia.[4] The children popped in and out of Charles's study, drawing on the backs of discarded manuscript sheets and gliding around on his wheeled stool. Charles used the stool for his microscope seat; he could wheel around to his desk to get a specimen, then roll back to his microscope, which he kept at the window for the best possible light. For the children, though, the stool was just fun.

A favorite game of all was sliding down the stairs on a board. Another favorite, usually played when the house was full of cousins, was a kind of loud hide-and-seek played all over the house, with lots of yelling. The children called it "roundabouts."[5]

From the time they were born, the Darwin children were surrounded by books, magazines, and newspapers. Charles and Emma were insatiable readers. They bought books. They borrowed books from libraries. They followed book reviews. And they read to their children—from a book of fairy tales Emma had kept from her own childhood, from Dickens's novels, and from other books. The children read too—

LIFE IN THE 1850s

For the first time the United States population (23 million in 1851, 3.2 million of whom were black slaves) exceeded that of England (20.8 million). It was still smaller than the populations of France (33 million), Germany (34 million), and China (430 million). Books of the decade included David Copperfield *by Charles Dickens (1850),* The Scarlet Letter *by Nathanial Hawthorne (1850),* Moby Dick *by Herman Melville (1851),* Uncle Tom's Cabin *by Harriet Beecher Stowe (1852),* Walden *by Henry David Thoreau (1854),* Leaves of Grass *by Walt Whitman (1855), and, finally,* On the Origin of Species *by Charles Darwin (1859). Isaac Singer invented the continuous stitch sewing machine in 1851, and Henry Steinway and his three sons opened their piano manufacturing company in 1853. England went to war again in 1854; the Crimean War would last until 1856. In the United States, the Republican Party was formed in 1854. In London, the National Portrait Gallery was founded in 1856, and the Victoria and Albert Museum opened in 1857. In 1859, a French tightrope walker named Charles Blondin crossed Niagara Falls on a tightrope. That same year, John Brown raided a federal arsenal at Harper's Ferry, West Virginia.*

HOUSEHOLD STAFF

Emma and Charles were very relaxed parents and gave their children a lot of freedom. It helped that there was plenty of staff: a butler, a footman, two gardeners, a cook, a kitchen maid, a laundry maid, a house-maid, and one or two nursery maids.[12] Jessie Brodie, whom everyone called Brodie, had been the children's nurse since 1842,[13] and in 1848 Emma had hired a governess, Miss Catherine Thorley.[14]

Gulliver's Travels, The Last of the Mohicans, the *Arabian Nights,* and other popular books of the time.[6]

Outside were sixteen acres of woods, lawn, gardens, and an orchard of apples, pears, quinces, and plums. Annie had a small garden of her own where she grew flowers and vegetables. There were a number of animals, including chickens and geese, cows, pigs, horses, a don-key, and an assortment of barn cats.[7]

Charles sometimes took one or two of the children on early morn-ing walks into the countryside.[8] On some days, the children joined their father at his work, counting the plant species in the meadow or following the paths of bumblebees. But Charles never tried to make his children like science. If they expressed interest, he was happy to teach them, but he didn't force his fascination with natural science on them. He wanted them to think for themselves.[9]

In addition to children, the house was often filled with guests. A steady stream of brothers and sisters, cousins, nieces, and nephews came to visit, as well as Charles's scientific friends from London.[10] Annie's favorite was Joseph Hooker, who often stayed for a week at a time, discussing science with her father, doing his own work at the din-ing room table, and playing with the children.

But in spite of the commotion, Charles Darwin was a man who valued and maintained peace and routine. In 1846, he had begun a study of barnacles that would continue for the next eight years. He rose early, appearing in the drawing room once in the morning to read the mail, again later on to read the newspaper, and then not until the end of the day. The rest of the time he could usually be found either walking the property (he did so several times a day) or behind his closed study door. His children said they could set the clock by the creak of the study door opening.[11]

Charles Darwin was a quiet, kind man, respected in both the sci-entific and local communities. He was a local magistrate, which meant that he was trusted to resolve small disputes among the citizenry. And, though his circle of close friends was small, it was strong. Charles was

TOP LEFT: THE DARWIN DRAW-
ING ROOM AT DOWN HOUSE

TOP RIGHT: DARWIN'S STUDY
AT DOWN HOUSE

BOTTOM LEFT: THE SANDWALK,
BUILT FOR DARWIN AT THE
REAR OF THEIR PROPERTY,
WHERE HE TOOK DAILY
STROLLS

a prodigious letter writer. Today 14,000 of his letters reside in libraries around the world; many more were lost or destroyed. In his correspondence, he shared information and ideas with his closest scientific friends and made inquiries of just about everyone else—farmers, military officers, gardeners, civil servants, zookeepers, and animal breeders from places as remote as India, China, New Zealand, and the United States—*anyone* who might have information he needed.[15] Between 1846 and 1854, while he was studying barnacles, he wrote to ship captains and traveling naturalists around the world and obtained barnacles from Australia to the Arctic.[16]

He also conducted studies closer to home. His barber raised pedigreed dogs—Charles interviewed him and took notes while he had his hair cut. Another old friend, a fellow hunter, knew a vast amount about breeding dogs and farm animals—Charles took lengthy notes on his ideas.

Darwin raised pigeons at Down House and belonged to several pigeon clubs. At one point he had a flock of ninety birds. He grew seeds in pots and experimented with flowers, observing everything with an eye toward finding evidence of adaptation. His studies of orchids led him to realize that the flowers and the insects that pollinated them must have evolved together.

CHAPTER 22

TRAGEDY

THROUGHOUT HIS LIFE, Charles Darwin suffered from headaches and nausea. Scholars have speculated as to the cause. Some have suggested that keeping his theory to himself for so long made him ill—he was all bottled up with thoughts of evolution he was afraid to share. Others have noted that he was often ill during times of family or work-related anxiety and speculated that his illnesses were stress related. Still others have suggested that Darwin might have contracted a chronic disease, perhaps while on his voyage. Whatever the cause, Darwin was frequently ill.

In 1842, James Manby Gully set up a hydrotherapy clinic in Malvern, England. Hydro- or water-therapy was the new rage in treatment of chronic illness, aches, or general malaise. It involved frequent showers and baths, the application of wet compresses, exercise, bland food, and spring water to drink.

In early 1849, after a sickly winter, Charles decided to try the treatment. The entire Darwin family, including all six children plus Miss Thorley (the governess) and maids, traveled to Malvern in March. There they rented a house not unlike Down House. While Charles took the water treatments, the children played in the field and woods next to the house, took dancing lessons on Fridays, and generally had a fine time.[1] They didn't return to Down House until June 30.

Charles felt the treatment was extremely beneficial. When he got home, he continued to follow some of the regimens, and over the years he would periodically return to Malvern or other hydrotherapy spas.[2]

IN THE MID-NINETEENTH CENTURY, it was the custom to send boys off to boarding schools while girls studied at home. In January 1850, the Darwins' oldest son, Willy, now ten, left Down House to study with the Reverend Mr. Wharton in Surrey.[3] Annie, who would be nine in March, was now the oldest child at home. She was a bright, open, affectionate child and the apple of her father's eye.

Annie loved the outdoors and spent as much time as she could swinging in the tree swing, caring for her own small garden, taking early morning walks her with father, exploring the countryside, wandering about the woods, romping in the orchard, and inventing games with her brothers and sisters and their playmates. As a young lady of the time, she also sewed and did embroidery and beadwork. She made clothes for her dolls and little decorations she called her "treasures." She had a small writing case covered in leather in which she kept stationery and matching envelopes, pens, and sealing wax, and she wrote letters to her cousins.[4] Annie had a gift for drawing and loved music and dancing. In fact, she seemed to take joy in everything, and everyone took joy in her.

But in July, Emma noticed that Annie did not seem well.[5] The nine-year-old and her sisters had had scarlet fever a year earlier in 1849, but they had recovered. What could be wrong?

By fall it was certain that Annie had some sort of illness, but the symptoms were vague. It was unclear to everyone what disease she might have.

In October of 1850, Charles decided to send Annie and her younger sister Etty with Miss Thorley to the seaside town of Ramsgate. Sea bathing was thought to be healthful, and he hoped the holiday would be good for Annie's health.

Ramsgate was an elegant resort town with beach chairs, umbrellas, donkey carts, and a festive atmosphere. The girls bathed in the ocean, collected shells, and generally enjoyed themselves. Two weeks later, Emma and Charles came to join them. But two days after her parents arrived, Annie developed a headache and fever, and the family returned to Down House.[6]

Annie recovered from her headache and fever, but though she wasn't forced to stay in bed, it was clear she wasn't truly well. Visits to the doctor in London weren't helping. As the months wore on, she didn't seem to get any better.

Annie's tenth birthday was on March 2, 1851. She felt quite well. Her brother Willy had come home from school the day before, and they played outside together. But the next week she came down with the flu. Charles decided to take her to the hydrotherapy clinic in Malvern. He hoped that Dr. Gully could help Annie with his water treatments. The whole family could not go along this time since Emma was pregnant again, but Charles took Etty and the children's nurse, Brodie, to keep Annie company. Emma, left behind at Down House while her sweet Annie was taken to Malvern to seek a cure, sat on the sofa and cried.[7]

ANNIE, THE DARWINS' SECOND CHILD, WHO DIED AT AGE TEN

Letters went back and forth by coach daily between Malvern and Down House. A letter mailed from Malvern by 6:30 p.m. would arrive at Down House around noon the next day. A letter sent by return mail from Down House would reach Malvern the next morning.[8]

For the first week, things seemed to go quite well. Miss Thorley, the governess, arrived early in April and found Annie and Etty happy and active.[9]

Then, suddenly, Annie had an attack of vomiting followed by a fever. When the fever broke, Dr. Gully felt the worst was over, though

Annie was by then very weak. But when he came to see her the next day, he could see that she was dangerously ill.[10]

Charles had returned to Down House, thinking that Annie had inherited his own chronic illness and was not in serious danger.[11] When he got the news of her worsening condition, he immediately hurried back to Malvern. Annie was very sick. "It is now from hour to hour a struggle between life and death," Charles wrote to Emma. "God only knows the issue."[12]

Once again Annie rallied. Charles sent word to Emma that Annie had had a quiet night and the greatest danger had passed.

Over the next few weeks, Annie grew weaker. She was alternately calm, delirious, calm again, then sick and vomiting. Her fever raged, then broke, then raged again. The letters flew back and forth between Charles and Emma, alternately hopeful and despairing. They were frantic.

On April 21, Annie seemed to rally. Her fever broke, and everyone was filled with hope. Two days later, on April 23, 1851, Annie died. She was ten years old.[13]

CHARLES WRITES ABOUT ANNIE

One week after her death, Charles set down several pages of his thoughts about his beloved daughter on black-bordered mourning paper. "From whatever point I look back at her, the main feature in her disposition which at once rises before me is her buoyant joyousness," he wrote. He remembered how she had loved to arrange his hair, "making it beautiful," or smooth his collar and cuffs. "Her joyousness and animal spirits radiated from her whole countenance and rendered every movement elastic and full of life and vigour. It was delightful and cheerful to behold her. Her dear face now rises before me, as she used sometimes to come running down stairs with a stolen pinch of snuff for me, her whole form radiant with the pleasure of giving pleasure. . . .

"We have lost the joy of the household, and the solace of our old age," he concluded. "She must have known how we loved her; oh, that she could now know how deeply, how tenderly we do still and shall ever love her dear joyous face. Blessings on her."[14]

At the time, the cause of Annie's death was described as a "fever." Today it is thought she probably died of tuberculosis.

Her father felt he had lost the joy of the household. He would mourn her for the rest of his life.

Emma carefully put Annie's "treasures" into her writing box, along with a map showing the location of her grave at Malvern and the daily notes Charles had taken at Annie's bedside. Annie's Box is a treasured heirloom in the Darwin family to this day.

ANNIE'S BOX, A COLLECTION OF MEMENTOS OF ANNIE KEPT IN HER WRITING BOX BY HER MOTHER, IS TODAY A TREASURED FAMILY HEIRLOOM.

CHAPTER 23

A MONTH OF NIGHTMARES

THOUGH DARWIN WOULD MISS his beloved Annie for the rest of his days, his work continued. By 1856, Charles had shared his thoughts about evolution by natural selection with only a few close friends. But "early in 1856," Charles wrote in his autobiography, "Lyell advised me to write out my views pretty fully, and I began at once to do so."[1] Darwin planned to title his book *Natural Selection*, and he was determined to make it as convincing as it could be. He had by then amassed such a bounty of evidence from the world that he hoped he would be able to persuade his fellow scientists that life has evolved through natural selection.

Two years later, in June 1858, he was more than halfway through writing the book, which he well knew to be the most important work of his life and his major contribution to science, when a package arrived from the Dutch East Indies. It was from Alfred Russel Wallace, a young naturalist who traveled the world collecting specimens and selling them to clients in England in order to further finance his travels. Charles had written to him several months earlier in the hope that Wallace could get him the skins of some Malayan poultry.

Inside the package was a short essay that laid out a theory of evolution by natural selection that was nearly identical to Darwin's own. Wallace even cited Malthus, whose *Essay on Population* had also inspired Darwin.

In a letter accompanying the essay, Wallace asked Charles to pass it along to Charles Lyell. He knew that Darwin and the eminent geologist were friends, and since Wallace's theory, like Darwin's own, drew on Lyell's *Principles of Geology*, he hoped it would be of interest to Sir Charles.

Darwin was flabbergasted. Somehow it had never occurred to him that anyone else might also come up with his natural selection theory. He felt sick at heart. All his years of painstaking work were suddenly for nothing. All his claims to his very own theory, to being the first with these groundbreaking ideas, were lost. All his hopes of making a major contribution to science were gone. In the scientific world, then as now, the first to publish gets the credit for the theory.

A less honorable man might have destroyed the essay, pretended not to have received it, and hurriedly gotten his own work into print. After all, Charles *had* come up with the idea first, many years ago; he just hadn't published it. He had delayed and worried, and now, here was a young man about to garner the acclaim and credit Charles had expected to be his own.

But Darwin didn't hesitate. The very next day he sent Wallace's essay on to Lyell. "I never saw a more striking coincidence," he wrote. "If Wallace had my M.S. sketch written out in 1842 he could not have made a better short abstract! Even his terms now stand as the Heads of my chapters."[2] He went on to say that he would, of course, send the paper to any journal Wallace wished.

Lyell, who immediately understood the similarity of Wallace's ideas to convictions Charles had long held, wrote back recommending that Darwin quickly publish something of his own.[3] But by then the Darwin family had other troubles. Etty, now fifteen, was stricken with a high fever. Charles and Emma were afraid she might have diphtheria, a deadly disease at the time. Then George's headmaster wrote to tell

ALFRED RUSSEL WALLACE

them that George had the measles, also a dangerous disease in 1858. With Etty so ill, they couldn't bring George home—he would have to be nursed at school. And the day after that frightening news, the baby, Charles Waring Darwin, then only nineteen months old, took ill.[4]

Distressed over his sick children, Charles would have liked to ignore the problem of Wallace's essay and his own publication plans altogether. He asked Charles Lyell to discuss the situation with Joseph Hooker, who was now director of the Royal Botanic Gardens at Kew. Perhaps they could find an honorable solution.[5]

Lyell and Hooker came up with a plan. They would present Alfred Wallace's essay *and* some of Charles's previous unpublished writings orally at the next meeting of the Linnean Society, a scientific society to which Lyell, Hooker, and Darwin all belonged. The papers would then be published.[6]

While Charles considered the plan he was distracted by further disaster at home. Baby Charles had become desperately ill with scarlet fever and was suffering terribly. Charles and Emma were anguished and at his bedside constantly, but they could not save him. He died on June 28.[7]

Grief-stricken, Charles wrote to Joseph Hooker on June 29, 1858. He enclosed his 1844 summary of the theory, written fourteen years earlier, with Hooker's own comments and questions written right on it. He also sent a copy of a letter he had written in 1857 to Asa Gray, professor of botany at Harvard University, in which he had laid out all the major points.[8] These papers would show that Darwin had documented his ideas years before Wallace wrote his essay.

Hooker's wife, Frances, copied sections of the 1844 summary and organized them so they could be read aloud, and on June 30, all the papers were delivered to the Society's secretary.[9]

The Linnean Society met on July 1, 1858. The papers were read in alphabetical order. This was the usual practice, but it served Darwin well that night. His 1844 summary came first, then his 1857 letter to Gray, and finally Wallace's 1858 essay. It could not be clearer that Charles Darwin had been the first to work out evolution through natural selection.[10]

Neither Charles Darwin nor Alfred Wallace were there to hear their work read. Wallace didn't even know his work was being presented.

A number of other papers were read at the evening meeting, and, perhaps due to the lateness of the hour by the time they had finished, no one lingered to discuss the Darwin/Wallace papers. In fact, no one seemed to pay them much heed at all. "This shows how necessary it is that any new view should be explained at considerable length in order to arouse public attention," Charles wrote in his autobiography.[11]

The papers were published in October 1858. But a few months later, the president of the Linnean Society, in summing up the year's events, remarked that nothing important had happened that year. History would prove him very wrong indeed.

CHILDHOOD DISEASES IN THE NINETEENTH CENTURY

The 1800s were not a safe century for children. People knew nothing about vitamins or antibiotics, and childhood diseases raged. In the 1830s nearly half the deaths in London were of children under age ten. In the United States, children were so used to seeing hearses on the streets that they made up a game they called Funerals.

Poor children often lived in homes without heat and drank water contaminated with sewage. Diarrhea and typhoid were the results.

Wealthy children fared better but were still in danger of pneumonia, bronchitis, tuberculosis, whooping cough, diphtheria, and smallpox. Scarlet fever raged in England from the 1840s through the 1870s. Measles outbreaks in 1863 and 1874 were even more deadly.

CHAPTER 24

THE ORIGIN OF
SPECIES

O F COURSE THEY HAD TO TELL Alfred Wallace what
they had done. It wasn't really proper to publish Wallace's
work without his permission. Charles had initially been
reluctant to publish his own papers beside Wallace's essay "as I
thought Mr. Wallace might consider my doing so unjustifiable."[1]

Charles and Joseph Hooker both wrote to Wallace, then Charles
took his family to recover on the Isle of Wight. He was still worried
about Etty's and George's health and mourning the death of baby
Charles. Now he was also brooding about what Wallace's reaction to
the presentation of his work might be. He needn't have worried.
Though Wallace was certainly surprised, he wrote back to *thank*
Hooker for including his essay in the Linnean Society presentation and
Journal. Wallace was a young man and not a recognized scientist, so
having his name associated with Darwin's could benefit him greatly.[2]
He also believed that Darwin deserved the credit, having come up with
the idea of evolution by natural selection first.

The beauty of the Isle of Wight was like a healthful tonic. As the children recovered in body, Charles began to recover in spirit. And he began to write. Hooker was pushing him to write another article for the Linnean Society *Journal*, and though Charles didn't think he could be brief enough, he began.

Home again at Down House in August, he kept on writing. After all the years of keeping silent, the Wallace business had opened the floodgates. Page after page flowed from Darwin's pen.[3] He didn't pick up where he had left off in June; he started fresh, incorporating pieces of what he had already written, but tightening it, honing his arguments, tying everything together more clearly. He felt he could see everything more clearly than ever before.

The manuscript grew and grew. And it was filled not with conjecture, but with facts. Charles had seen, with his own eyes, in the oceans, on the islands, in the mountains, and on the plains he had explored, the evidence of evolution by natural selection at work on living creatures. All of his observations, so carefully noted over so many years, would now help him to persuade his readers.

Thirteen months after he began, in May 1859, Charles Darwin finished the book we know as *The Origin of Species,* a book that would transform the study and understanding of biology. It was written in an easy, accessible style. Darwin wrote it not only to be read by the scientific community, but by the educated public as well.

Charles Darwin tried to explain how evolution has affected all forms of life with one large exception: human beings. He wasn't yet ready to face the reaction to that idea, though he would do so later in his book *Descent of Man.* He also tried to answer the doubts and criticisms he expected some readers to have. "I had . . . followed a golden rule," he wrote in his autobiography, "namely, that whenever a published fact, a new observation or thought came across me, which was opposed to my general results, to make a memorandum of it without fail and at once." In this way, Charles was able to address the objections he expected to be raised. Of the biggest objection, though, he wrote nothing: he did not mention God.[4]

THE MYSTERY OF MYSTERIES

"When on board the H.M.S. *Beagle,* as naturalist, I was much struck with certain facts," Darwin wrote in the opening paragraph of his Introduction to *The Origin of Species.* "These facts seemed to me to throw some light on the origin of species—that mystery of mysteries, as it has been called by one of our greatest philosophers." That great philosopher was, of course, Sir John Herschel, whom Charles had visited in Cape Town.

At around 500 pages, the manuscript of *The Origin of Species* was much too long for publication in a scientific journal. But who would publish it in book form? Charles consulted Lyell. Might his own publisher, John Murray, be interested? Murray, who had published the second edition of Darwin's *Journal of Researches*, agreed even before reading it. When he did read it, he thought the theory was absurd,[5] but he published it anyway.

In 1859, publishing houses did not edit their authors' work. Any corrections, clarifications, or polishing was done by the author and his or her friends. Charles Lyell read the printer's proofs carefully and made suggestions. Emma worked with Charles on the clarity of his language. Frances Hooker did the same, as did Emma's friend Georgina Tollet.[6]

On his publisher's recommendation, Charles changed the title of his book from *An Abstract of an Essay on the Origin of Species and Varieties Through Natural Selection* to *The Origin of Species by Means of Natural Selection, or the Preservation of Favoured Races in the Struggle for Life*.[7] Fortunately the long title was eventually whittled down to size.

On October 1, 1859, Charles turned in the corrected proofs of *The Origin of Species*. On October 2, he checked into a hydrotherapy clinic in the town of Ilkley. He was ill and worn out.[8]

CHARLES DARWIN'S WRITING PROCESS

"With my larger books I spend a good deal of time over the general arrangement of the matter," Charles Darwin wrote of his writing habits. "I first make the rudest outline in two or three pages, and then a larger one in several pages." He then enlarged upon each item in the outline, often transforming it altogether. He kept from thirty to forty large folders into which he put facts as he found them. "I have bought many books," he continued, "and at their ends I make an index of all the facts that concern my work."

"I have as much difficulty as ever in expressing myself clearly and concisely; and this difficulty has caused me a very great loss of time," wrote Darwin toward the end of his life, "but it has had the compensating advantage of forcing me to think long and intently about every sentence, and thus I have been often led to see errors in reasoning."[9]

The Origin of Species was published on November 24, 1859, and sold out its first edition that same day. Murray had printed only 1,250 copies, but their rapid sale was enough to please both Charles and his publisher.[10] The second printing would be 3,000 copies, more than twice that of the first. By 1876, the book had sold more than 16,000 copies in England and had been translated into almost every European language. "Even an essay in Hebrew has appeared on it, showing that the theory is contained in the Old Testament!" Darwin wrote.[11]

Readers' reactions to the book ran to extremes. Darwin's scientific friends were awestruck. Though they knew something of his theory, they had no idea of the grand scope of his thinking. Even when they did not agree, they could still respect the power and beauty of his argument.[12] Biologist Thomas H. Huxley greatly admired Darwin's theory and was eager to defend it. "How extremely stupid not to have thought of that!" he wrote to Charles.[13] Erasmus wrote his brother that "For myself I really think it is the most interesting book I ever read, & can only compare it to the first knowledge of chemistry, getting into a new world or rather behind the scenes."[14]

Religious thinkers, however, including Adam Sedgwick, were furious. It was blasphemous to think that any new species had been created by any means other than directly by God![15] A notable exception among the clergy was Reverend Charles Kingsley, who wrote to tell Darwin he could easily imagine God setting the plan in motion, then allowing adaptation to proceed on its own. Rev. Kingsley's letter was quoted in the second edition of Darwin's book.[16]

The controversy generated by the book wasn't really over evolution. Evolution had been discussed and argued about for years; even Charles's own grandfather had speculated about it. What made Darwin's work revolutionary was that he could explain how species can change: by natural selection. *Natural,* not divine selection. No

THOMAS HENRY HUXLEY, WHO WAS CALLED DARWIN'S "BULLDOG"

mention was made of a Creator; Darwin's evidence showed that natural processes produced changes in species. And he had amassed a mountain of facts to back up his explanation of the process. The controversy over his theory would continue for the rest of Darwin's life and certainly would not end after his death; in fact, it continues to this day.

Darwin was not surprised by the uproar. In fact, he expected it and had dreaded it for many years before publication. "I remember when in Good Success Bay, in Tierra del Fuego, thinking (and I believe that I wrote home to the effect) that I could not employ my life better than in adding a little to natural science," he would later write in his autobiography. "This I have done to the best of my abilities, and critics may say what they like, but they cannot destroy this conviction."[17] Charles put his faith in the future. As he wrote in *The Origin*, "I look with confidence to the future, to young and rising naturalists, who will be able to view both sides of the question with impartiality."[18]

Charles Darwin, the boy who was fascinated by beetles, the seasick young man on a five-year ocean voyage, the geologist who marveled at how mountains were made, the naturalist who studied living creatures of all sorts, gave us a glimpse into the amazing workings of life itself. "There is grandeur in this view of life," he wrote. "From so simple a beginning endless forms most beautiful and most wonderful have been, and are being, evolved."[19]

EPILOGUE

Aftr publication of *The Origin of Species*, Charles Darwin went on to live a quiet life. In 1871, he wrote *Descent of Man*, making it clear that human beings have also evolved, something he had barely hinted at in *The Origin*. His scientific curiosity never waned. He studied carnivorous plants that eat insects. He investigated how climbing plants climb. He experimented with earthworms, at one time placing a bowl of earthworms on the piano to see if and how they would react when the piano was played.

The study of worms was Darwin's last major project. He died quietly of heart disease at Down House on April 19, 1882, at age 73. He was laid to rest in Westminster Abbey, taking his place among kings and queens, great writers and poets—England's most revered sons and daughters.

Charles Darwin has been called the most important figure in the history of biology. In a recent poll, his countrymen voted him among the top three figures in British history. They are enormously proud of his great scientific achievement.

Yet Darwin was right to worry about the negative reactions to his evolutionary ideas. His old Cambridge geology professor, the Reverend Adam Sedgwick, was especially scathing in his attack on Darwin's *Origin of Species*. While Thomas Huxley ("Darwin's Bulldog") argued

OPPOSITE:
CHARLES ROBERT DARWIN
IN OLD AGE

passionately in favor of *The Origin*, Bishop Samuel ("Soapy Sam") Wilberforce argued just as passionately against. Their Oxford debate was followed avidly in the popular press, which also ran cartoons portraying Darwin as an ape. And while the Church of England and other Christian and Jewish sects in Britain did not officially denounce evolution, the theory was considered heretical in many congregations.

The situation grew even worse in the United States—where Darwin had once thought he might move to escape the religious backlash he faced at home! In the early years of the twentieth century, Christian Fundamentalism became widely popular. Among the core beliefs of the Fundamentalist movement is the insistence on the literal truth of every word in the Bible, including the account of Creation as it is written in the book of Genesis. Fundamentalists in many states, especially those in the South and West, began to fight for laws that would forbid the teaching of anything that contradicted their understanding of the Bible, specifically the teaching of evolution. These laws were called "monkey laws" in the mistaken belief that Darwin had claimed that humans descended from monkeys. In fact, Darwin's theory showed that this was not the case at all.

In 1925, John Scopes, a high school biology teacher in Dayton, Tennessee, was convicted of violating such a law, the Butler Act, by teaching evolution. Scopes's conviction was overturned by a State Court of Appeals, but since it was never ruled on by the U.S. Supreme Court, monkey laws like Tennessee's remained on the books for decades. The teaching of evolution in the United Sates fell into a sort of "dark ages," all but disappearing from textbooks until 1957, when the Russians launched the first artificial space satellite, "Sputnik." Suddenly the United States realized in horror that it had fallen behind the rest of the world in science and technology.

Fundamentalists fought against the reappearance of evolution in American high schools. They argued to give something they called "scientific creationism" equal time with the study of evolution in the school curriculum. "Scientific creationism" proposed that the Earth is only

10,000 years old and that species are created independently and do not change once they have been created. The Fundamentalists insisted that these claims were supported by science, not by the Bible. This time the courts weighed in on the side of science. The U.S. Supreme Court ruled that such "equal time" laws were as invalid as the older monkey laws had been: both violated the separation of church and state mandated by the U.S. Constitution.

Most recently, Fundamentalists have proposed a theory of Intelligent Design, which maintains that organisms are too complex to have been formed by natural processes such as mutation and natural selection. The proponents of Intelligent Design also claim that their conclusions are based on science—but they offer no testable hypotheses and no scientific support for their theory.

The controversy over Darwin's writings rages on. Sometimes people object that evolution is "only a theory," as though there is a scale of credibility with "fact" on top, "theory" somewhere in the middle, and "lie" at the bottom. In science, however, all the important ideas are theories. Scientific theories never *become* facts, they *explain* facts. This is an important distinction that many people do not understand. Facts do not change. Theories that explain how and why the facts are what they are can change.

A scientific theory enables scientists to make predictions about how something will behave. The more accurate those predictions prove to be, the sounder the theory becomes. Gravity is a theory—but no one doubts its truth when they see an apple fall. And before there was a theory to explain why apples fall, the fact remained that they did. The existence and nature of atoms is a theory. So are plate tectonics, quantum mechanics, and Einstein's theory of relativity.

Scientific theories are built on vast accumulations of solid evidence, observation, and experimentation. This does not mean we do not continue to test these theories. Charles Darwin taught us how to test the idea of evolution by natural selection through careful observation of nature. The changes produced through evolution are there to be seen in both fossils and living species. The same sorts of clues that gave Darwin the idea more than a century ago are there for us to see today. For nearly 150 years since the publication of *The Origin of Species*, people have been finding and recording the same patterns of evolutionary change over and over again. When a theory is tested so thoroughly, and found to make accurate predictions again and again, we lose our doubt about its truth.

We can see evolution in action. When attacked by man-made drugs, viruses and bacteria mutate into forms not affected by the drugs. Only those with resistance to the drugs can survive, and the resistant organisms reproduce. That's natural selection we can see right in front of us.

Everything we have learned in biology since Darwin—about DNA, for example—reinforces his conclusions. Discoveries in other areas of science, such as carbon dating, provide further confirmation. Many branches of science, from biology to geology to anthropology and genetics, cannot be understood except through an understanding of the process of evolution. Evolution by natural selection is a theory, yes—but it is one of the most powerful theories ever proposed in modern science.

TIMELINE OF CHARLES DARWIN ON THE H.M.S. *BEAGLE*

1831

December 27   The *Beagle* sets sail from Plymouth, England

1832

January 16–February 8   Cape Verde Islands

February 16   St. Paul's Rocks, 540 miles off the coast of Brazil

February 20   Island of Fernando de Noronha

February 29–March 18   Bahia (Salvador), Brazil

April 4–July 5   Rio de Janeiro

While the Beagle *sails up and down the Brazilian coast checking charts, Darwin explores on land.*

July 26–August 19   Montevideo

September 6–October 17   Bahía Blanca

November 2–26   Montevideo

December 16–February 26, 1833   Tierra del Fuego

1833

March 1–April 6   Falkland Islands

April 28–July 23   Maldonado

August 3   Arrive at Patagones at the mouth of the Río Negro

August 11–17   Land trip from Patagones to Bahía Blanca

August 24–October 6   Surveying the Argentinian coast

September 8–20   Land trip from Bahía Blanca to Buenos Aires

September 27–October 2   Land trip to Santa Fe and along the Río Paraná

October 21–December 6   Montevideo

November 14–28   Land trip to Mercedes, Uruguay

December 23–January 4, 1834   Port Desire

1834

January	Strait of Magellan
January 9–19	Port St. Julian
January 29–March 7	Tierra del Fuego
March 10–April 7	Falkland Islands
May–June	Strait of Magellan
June 28–July 13	Chiloé
July 23–November 10	Valparaíso
August 14–September 27	Land trip in the Andes
November 21–February 2, 1835	Chiloé and Chronos archipelago

1835

February 8–22	Valdivia
March 4–7	Concepción
March 11–April 27	Valparaíso
March 13–April 10	Land trip to Santiago, then across the Andes
June 22–July 4	Copiapó
July 12–15	Iquique, Peru
July 19–September 6	Callao
September 15–October 20	Galapagos Islands
November 15–26	Tahiti
December 21–30	New Zealand

1836

January 12–30	Sydney, Australia
February 15–17	Hobart, Tasmania
March 6–14	King George Sound
April 1–12	Keeling Islands
April 24–May 9	Mauritius
May 31–June 15	Cape of Good Hope
July 8–14	St. Helena
July 19–23	Ascension Island
August 1–6	Bahia (Salvador), Brazil
September 20–24	Azores
October 2	Falmouth, Cornwall, England

TIMELINE OF CHARLES DARWIN'S LIFE AND TIMES

February 12, 1809   Charles Darwin is born

Abraham Lincoln is born

1812   The U.S. declares war on Britain

Publication of *Children's and Household Tales* by the Brothers Grimm

Beethoven finishes his seventh and eighth symphonies

1815   Napolean is defeated at Waterloo

The 1812 War ends

The Underground Railroad is started to help slaves escape

1816   The kaleidoscope and the stethoscope are invented

1817   Charles's mother dies

1818   Charles starts at Dr. Butler's School

Publication of *Frankenstein* by Mary Wollstonecraft Shelley

1819   Charles visits Wales for three weeks, where he finds insects he has never seen before

1824   The Erie Canal is completed

1825   Charles begins his studies at Edinburgh

1826   Charles joins the Plinian Society

1828   Charles arrives at Cambridge in January and meets John Steven Henslow

Publication of *The American Dictionary of the English Language* by Noah Webster

1829   Publication of *The Three Musketeers* by Alexander Dumas

1830   Publication of Volume I of *Principles of Geology* by Charles Lyell

1831   Invention of chloroform

London Bridge opens

First horse-drawn buses appear in New York

August: Charles accompanies geologist Adam Sedgwick to Wales

September 1: Charles accepts Captain FitzRoy's offer to sail on the *Beagle*

December 27: The *Beagle* sets sail

1834   Abraham Lincoln enters politics as an assemblyman in the Illinois legislature

1835   Hans Christian Andersen publishes his first children's stories

September 15: Charles arrives in the Galapagos Islands

October 20: Charles departs Galapagos Islands

1836   May: Charles meets Sir John Herschel in Cape Town

March 6: Davy Crocket is killed at the Alamo

Publication of the first botany textbook: *Elements of Botany* by Asa Gray

October 2: The *Beagle* returns to England

1837	Victoria becomes Queen of England
	March 7: Charles moves in with his brother Ras
	July: Charles begins work on his species theory
1838	October: Charles reads *Essay on Population* by Thomas Malthus
	November 11: Charles proposes to Emma
1839	January 29: Charles and Emma marry
	The first bicycle is built, in Scotland
	The First Opium War begins between Britain and China (the Opium Wars end in 1842)
	Publication of *The Journal of a Naturalist*
	December 27: William Erasmus Darwin, the Darwins' first child, is born
1840	Publication of *Zoology of the Voyage of the Beagle*
1841	March 2: Anne Elizabeth Darwin (Annie) is born
	Hypnosis is discovered by Scottish surgeon James Braid
	The first university degrees are granted to women in America
1842	The Darwins move to Down House
	Publication of *The Structure & Distribution of Coral Reefs*
	June: Charles writes out a short summary of his species theory
	September 25: Mary Eleanor Darwin is born
	October 16: Mary Eleanor Darwin dies
	Ether is first used for surgery
	November 4: Abraham Lincoln marries Mary Todd
1843	September 25: Henrietta Emma Darwin (Etty) is born
	Charles meets Joseph Hooker
	Publication of *A Christmas Carol* by Charles Dickens
	Sequoia creates the Cherokee alphabet
1844	Charles's species theory is now 230 pages; he instructs Emma to publish it after his death
	Morse's telegraph is used for the first time
1845	July 9: Goerge Howard Darwin is born
1846	Charles begins his study of barnacles; it will continue for eight years
	The Smithsonian Institution is founded in Washington, D.C.
	Irish potato famine begins
1847	July 8: Elizabeth Darwin (Betty) is born
	The Gold Rush begins in the U.S.
1848	August 16: Francis Darwin is born
	Invention of the safety match
1849	Publication of *David Copperfield* by Charles Dickens
1850	January 15: Leonard Darwin is born
1851	April 24: Annie Darwin dies at age 10

	May 13: Horace Darwin is born
	Publication of *Moby Dick* by Herman Melville
	September 18: the first *New York Times*
1852	Publication of *Uncle Tom's Cabin* by Harriet Beecher Stowe
1854	The Republican Party is formed in the U.S.
	The Crimean War begins
1856	**Charles begins to write *Natural Selection*, which will become *The Origin of Species***
	December 6: Charles Waring Darwin is born
1857	The Victoria and Albert Museum and the National Portrait Gallery open in London
1858	**June: Charles receives Alfred Russel Wallace's essay that mirrors his own thought**
	June 28: Baby Charles Waring Darwin dies
	July 1: Darwin's 1844 summary of his theory and Wallace's 1858 essay are read aloud at the Linnean Society; the papers are published in October
1859	Work on the Suez Canal begins (-1869)
	June 30: Charles Blondin crosses Niagara Falls on tightrope
	October 16: John Brown raids Harper's Ferry
	November 24: *The Origin of Species* is published
1860	November 6: Abraham Lincoln is elected the 16th President of the United States
1861	April 12: The Civil War begins with the Confederate attack on Fort Sumter, South Carolina
1862	**Publication of *Fertilisation of Orchids***
	September 22: The Emancipation Proclamation is passed
1865	April 9: Lee surrenders to Grant at Appomattox
	April 14: Abraham Lincoln is assassinated
1868	**Publication of *Variation of Animals & Plants Under Domestication***
	Publication of *Little Women* by Louisa May Alcott
	The game of badminton is invented in England
1869	The first postcards are introduced in Austria
1871	**Publication of *The Descent of Man***
	P. T. Barnum opens his circus
1872	**Publication of *The Expression of Emotions in Man & Animals***
	Brooklyn Bridge opens
	Publication of *Around the World in 80 Days* by Jules Verne
1874	The first impressionist exhibition is held in Paris
	The first American zoo in established in Philadelphia
1875	Publication of *The Adventures of Tom Sawyer* by Mark Twain
1876	**Publication of *Effects of Cross and Self Fertilsation in the Vegetable Kingdom***
	Invention of the telephone by Alexander Graham Bell
1882	**April 19: Charles Darwin dies at age 73**

NOTES

Abbreviations

AMNH: Darwin Exhibition Notes, American Museum of Natural History, October 19, 2005.

Voyaging: Browne, Janet. 1995. *Charles Darwin. Voyaging.* Princeton: Princeton University Press.

Autobiography: Barlow, Nora, ed. 1958. *The Autobiography of Charles Darwin 1809-1882 with original omissions restored.* London: Collins. Norton Paperback Edition 1969.

Desmond and Moore: Desmond, A., and J. Moore. 1991. *Darwin. The Life of a Tormented Evolutionist.* New York: W.W. Norton.

Beagle: Darwin, Charles. 1839. *Voyage of the* Beagle. London: Henry Colburn. Edition quoted © Janet Browne and Michael Neve, eds., 1989, New York and London: Penguin Books, Penguin Classic paperback edition.

Keynes: Keynes, Randal. 2001. *Darwin, His Daughter & Human Evolution.* New York: Riverhead Books. Trade Paperback Edition. First published in England by Fourth Estate Limited as *Annie's Box. Charles Darwin, His Daughter and Human Evolution.*

Letters: Darwin, Fancis, ed. *The Life of Charles Darwin 1809-1882 Including His Letters & An Autobiographical Chapter* 200th Birthday Commemorative Edition, Revised and Reedited by J.P. de Boulogny, © 2008 J.P. de Boulogny.

Power of Place: Browne, Janet. 2002. *Charles Darwin. The Power of Place.* New York: Alfred A. Knopf. Edition cited: Princeton: Princeton University Press. Trade Paperback Edition.

Origin: Darwin, Charles. 1859. *The Origin of Species.* Gramercy Edition 1979. New York: Random House.

Cosmos: Helferich, Gerard. 2004. *Humboldt's Cosmos.* New York, Gotham Books.

Correspondence: F.H. Burkhardt, S. Smith, et. al., eds. 1983-94. *The Correspondence of Charles Darwin.* Vols. 1-9 (1821-61). Cambridge: Cambridge University Press.

Quammen: Quammen, David. 2006. *The Reluctant Mr. Darwin.* New York: Atlas Books, W.W. Norton & Company.

Emma Darwin: H.E. Litchfield, ed. 1904. *Emma Darwin, wife of Charles Darwin: a century of family letters.* 2 vols. Cambridge: privately printed.

Chapter 1
A Naturalist Is Born

1 Voyaging p xi, quoting from *The life and letters of Charles Darwin,* Francis Darwin, ed. 1887. 3 vols. London.
2 Autobiography pp 22–23.
3 Autobiography pp 26–27.
4 Autobiography p 27.
5 Autobiography p 22.
6 Autobiography p 23.
7 Voyaging p 14, from private collection.
8 AMNH pp 10, 19.

Chapter 2
School Days

1 Autobiography p 22.
2 Autobiography p 42.
3 Autobiography p 27.
4 Autobiography p 45.
5 Autobiography p 45.
6 Autobiography p 28.
7 Autobiography p 28.

Chapter 3
Edinburgh

1 Autobiography p 47.
2 Autobiography p 47.

3 Autobiography p 48.
4 Autobiography p 49.
5 Autobiography p 51.g
6 Autobiography p 46.
7 Autobiography pp 53–54.

Chapter 4
Cambridge

1 Autobiography p 56.
2 Autobiography p 57.
3 Autobiography p 61.
4 Autobiography p 62.
5 Letter from Charles Darwin to William Darwin Fox, June 30, 1828, Masters and Fellows of

Christ's College, Cambridge.
6 Autobiography p 62.
7 Autobiography p 63.
8 Autobiography p 62.
9 Autobiography p 58.
10 Autobiography p 64.
11 Autobiography p 64.
12 Autobiography pp 64–65.
13 Autobiography p 68.

Chapter 5
Summer 1831

1 Cosmos pp 38–42.
2 Voyaging p 136.
3 Autobiography p 60.
4 Voyaging p 138.
5 Autobiography p 69.
6 Autobiography pp 69–70.
7 Letters p107.
8 Autobiography p 71.

Chapter 6
A Curious Turn of Events

1 Autobiography p 71.
2 Autobiography p 71.
3 Autobiography p 71.
4 Autobiography p 72.
5 Voyaging pp 159–60.
6 Letters p 86.
7 Autobiography pp 79–80.
8 Autobiography pp 72–73.

Chapter 7
Under Way at Last

1 Desmond and Moore p 108.
2 Letter from Charles Darwin to Robert Darwin, February 8–March 1, 1832, English Heritage (Down House).
3 Beagle p 41.
4 Beagle p 44.
5 Beagle p 44.
6 Beagle p 45.

Chapter 8
Crossing the Atlantic

1 AMNH p 62.
2 Beagle p 50.

3 AMNH p 76.

Chapter 9
Rio de Janeiro

1 Beagle p 69.
2 Letter from Charles Darwin to J.S. Henslow, May 18–June 16, 1832, Archives of the Royal Botanic Gardens, Kew, Folio 12; in volume of letters from Charles Darwin to Professor Henslow 1831–1837.
3 Beagle p 63.
4 Beagle pp 66–67.
5 Beagle p 67.
6 Beagle p 67.
7 Voyaging p 215.
8 Beagle pp 64–65.
9 Beagle p 69.
10 AMNH p 43.

Chapter 10
Land of the Giants

1 Beagle p 76.
2 Beagle p 78.
3 Beagle p 79.
4 Beagle p 76.
5 Beagle pp 105–6.
6 Letter from Robert FitzRoy to Francis Beaufort, August 15, 1832, The National Archives, U.K.

Chapter 11
Tierra del Fuego

1 Beagle p 174.
2 Voyaging p 238.
3 Beagle p 180.
4 Voyaging p 252.
5 Voyaging pp 252–3.

Chapter 12
Galloping North

1 Beagle pp 88–89.
2 Beagle p 90.
3 Voyaging p 259.
4 Beagle p 111.

5 Beagle p 127.
6 Beagle p 135.
7 Voyaging pp 228–9.
8 Beagle p 136.
9 Beagle p 141.
10 Beagle p 142.

Chapter 13
Eating the Evidence

1 Beagle p 155.

Chapter 14
The Fuegian Experiment

1 Desmond and Moore p 148.
2 Beagle p 185.
3 AMNH p 68.
4 AMNH p 61.
5 Beagle p 204.

Chapter 15
Explosions

1 Beagle p 205.
2 Beagle p 207.
3 Voyaging pp 281–2.
4 Beagle p 228.
5 Beagle p 237.
6 Voyaging p 286.
7 Beagle p 238.
8 Beagle p 239.

Chapter 16
Into the Andes

1 Beagle p 247.
2 Beagle p 248.
3 Beagle p 249.
4 Beagle p 253.

Chapter 17
The Galapagos

1 Voyaging p 297.
2 Voyaging p 298.
3 Beagle p 277.
4 Beagle pp 278–9.
5 Beagle p 287.

Chapter 18
Sailing Home

1   Beagle p 313.
2   Charles Darwin's "Ornithological Notes," June 1836, page 74 of 85, The Syndics of Cambridge University Library.

Chapter 19
Home at Last

1   Voyaging pp 321–22.
2   Voyaging pp 335–37.
3   Quammen, pp 21–23.
4   Autobiography p 83.
5   Autobiography pp 83–84.
6   Autobiography p 83.

Chapter 20
Family Life and Human Evolution

1   List made by Charles Darwin, July 1838, The Syndics of Cambridge University Library DAR 210.10.
2   Emma Darwin 1:418–20 as cited in Voyaging p 391.
3   Letter from Charles Darwin to Emma Wedgwood, January 20, 1839, The Syndics of Cambridge University Library DAR 210.19.
4   Correspondence 5:542 as cited in Voyaging p 393.
5   Keynes p 10.
6   Keynes p 8.
7   Keynes p 16.
8   Voyaging pp 424–30.
9   Voyaging p 433.
10   Keynes p 69.
11   Keynes p 70.
12   Power of Place p 6.
13   Voyaging p 444.
14   Voyaging pp 446–47.
15   Letter from Charles Darwin to Joseph Hooker, January 11, 1844, The Syndics of Cambridge University Library DAR 114.1:3.
16   Voyaging pp 461–70.

Chapter 21
Life at Down House

1   Keynes p 105.
2   Keynes p 102.
3   Keynes p 101.
4   Voyaging p 531.
5   Keynes p 107.
6   Keynes pp 115–117.
7   Keynes p 107.
8   Keynes p 112.
9   Keynes p 123.
10   Voyaging p 531.
11   Voyaging p 497.
12   Keynes p 84.
13   Keynes p 87.
14   Keynes p 126.
15   Power of Place p 11.
16   Voyaging p 483.

Chapter 22
Tragedy

1   Keynes pp 171–72.
2   Voyaging pp 493–95.
3   Keynes p 179.
4   Keynes p 133.
5   Keynes p 181.
6   Keynes pp 184–87.
7   Keynes p 195.
8   Keynes p 197.
9   Keynes p 202.
10   Keynes pp203–04.
11   Keynes p 197.
12   Keynes p 205.
13   Voyaging pp 498–501.
14   Keynes pp 237–240.

Chapter 23
A Month of Nightmares

1   Autobiography p 121.
2   Letter from Charles Darwin to Charles Lyell, June 26, 1858, page 1 of 4, American Philosophical Society.
3   Power of Place p 14.
4   Power of Place p 13.
5   Power of Place p 14.
6   Power of Place p 35.
7   Power of Place p 36.
8   Power of Place p 38.
9   Power of Place p 40.
10   Power of Place p 40.
11   Autobiography p 122.

Chapter 24
The Origin of Species

1   Autobiography p 121.
2   Power of Place pp 43-46.
3   Power of Place pp 46-47.
4   Power of Place pp 59-60.
5   Power of Place p 75.
6   Power of Place pp 76–77.
7   Power of Place p 81.
8   Power of Place p 81.
9   Autobiography p 137.
10   Power of Place p 88.
11   Autobiography p 123.
12   Power of Place pp 90–91.
13   Letter from Thomas Huxley to Charles Darwin, November 23, 1859, page 5 of 6, The Syndics of Cambridge University Library DAR 98 (ser.2): 11–13.
14   Letter from Erasmus Darwin to Charles Darwin, November 23, 1859, page 3 of 4, The Syndics of Cambridge University Library DAR 98 (ser. 2): 14–15.
15   Power of Place pp 93–94.
16   Power of Place p 95.
17   Autobiography p 126.
18   Origin p 453.
19   Origin pp 459–60.

LIST OF ILLUSTRATIONS

All illustrations used by permission

Tree of Life, reproduced by the kind permission of the Syndics of Cambridge University Library, p. vi

Josiah Wedgwood II, 326868: American Museum of Natural History (hereafter AMNH), p. 2

Erasmus Darwin, #326798: AMNH Special Collections, p. 4

Jean-Baptiste Lamarck, #124768: AMNH Special Collections, p. 5

Young Charles and Catherine Darwin, #326676: AMNH Special Collections, p. 7

Robert Waring Darwin, #326712: AMNH Special Collections, p.8

Susannah Wedgwood Darwin, #125315: AMNH Special Collections, p. 9

Zoonomia title page, Department of Library Services, AMNH, p. 14

John James Audubon, courtesy of the Museum of Science, Boston, p. 15

"Go it Charlie" cartoon, reproduced by the kind permission of the Syndics of Cambridge University Library, p. 19

John Stevens Henslow, #326670: AMNH Special Collections, p. 20

Adam Sedgwick, #326700: AMNH Special Collections, p. 24

Captain Robert FitzRoy, #326705: AMNH Special Collections, p. 28

Charles Lyell, AMNH Special Collections, p. 31

Drawings of the H.M.S. Beagle, #327357: AMNH Special Collections, p. 32, 33

Crossing the equator, Department of Library Services, AMNH, p. 37

Capybaras, Department of Library Services, AMNH, p. 44

Darwin's rhea by John Gould, Department of Library Services, AMNH, p. 45

Fossil Glyptotherium, Department of Library Services, AMNH, p. 47

Patagonian tableau, Department of Library Services, AMNH, p. 48

The Fuegians, Department of Library Services, AMNH, p. 51

Megatherium skeleton, #2A4479: AMNH Special Collections, p. 54

Toxodon skeleton, Department of Library Services, AMNH, p. 56

Toxodon skull, Department of Library Services, AMNH, p. 57

Beached Beagle, Department of Library Services, AMNH, p. 60

Strait of Magellan, Department of Library Services, AMNH, p. 62

Ruined Concepción cathedral, Department of Library Services, AMNH, p. 66

Galapagos penguins, Niles Eldredge, p. 72

Galapagos Tortoise Top, Department of Library Services, AMNH, p. 73

Galapagos Tortoises Bottom, Ted Lewin, p. 73

Marine Iguana, Niles Eldredge, p. 74

Land Iguana, Ted Lewin, p. 75

Some Galapagos islands, Department of Library Services, AMNH, p. 76

Mockingbirds, Hood Island, Ted Lewin, p. 77

John Herschel, #2A3376: AMNH Special Collections, p. 80

Drawing of finches by John Gould, Department of Library Services, AMNH, p. 83

Richard Owen, #28002: AMNH Special Collections, p. 85

Portraits of Emma and Charles Darwin in 1840, Down House, Downe, Kent, UK/Bridgeman Art Library, p. 90

Jenny the orangutan, The British Library, p. 92

Charles and William Darwin, #326799: AMNH Special Collections, p. 94

Joseph Hooker, #326880: AMNH Special Collections, p. 95

The Queen's Head Pub, Niles Eldredge, p. 98

Down House from the rear, Niles Eldredge, p. 98

Down House greenhouse, Niles Eldredge, p. 98

Church at Downe, Niles Eldredge, p. 98

Down House drawing room, Jonathan Bailey/English Heritage Photo Library, p. 101

Darwin's study, Nigel Corrie/English Heritage Photo Library, p. 101

The Sandwalk, Niles Eldredge, p. 101

Annie, English Heritage Photo Library, p. 105

Annie's box, Angelo Hornak, p. 107

Alfred Russel Wallace, AMNH Special Collections, p. 110

Thomas Henry Huxley, #326882: AMNH Special Collections, p. 115

Charles Darwin in old age, AMNH Special Collections, p. 118

Darwin in 1854, AMNH Special Collections, p. 135

British ten-pound note, p. 136

FURTHER READING

A Selected Bibliography of Books for Young People about Charles Darwin and his Voyage on the Beagle

The Adventures of Charles Darwin by Peter Ward, Cambridge University Press 1986, ages 9-12, 107 pages

Animals Charles Darwin Saw: An Around-the-World Adventure by Sandra Markle, illustrated by Zina Saunders, Chronicle 2009, ages 7-10, 48 pages

Charles and Emma: The Darwins' Leap of Faith by Deborah Heiliman, Holt 2008, ages 12-up, 272 pages

Charles Darwin by David C. King, DK Children 2006, ages 9-12, 128 pages

Charles Darwin by Alan Gibbons, illustrated by Leo Brown, told from the point of view of a ten-year-old apprentice aboard the *Beagle*, Kingfisher 2008, ages 6-10, 64 pages

Charles Darwin and the Evolution Revolution by Rebecca Stefoff, Oxford Universtiy Press, USA 1996, YA, 128 pages

Charles Darwin and the Origin of the Species by Jim Whiting, Mitchell Lane Publishers 2005, ages 9-12, 48 pages

Charles Darwin and the Theory of Evolution by Heather Adamson, illustrated by Gordon Purcell and Al Milgrom, Capstone Press (Graphic Library) 2007, ages 9-12, 32 pages

Darwin by Alice B. McGinty, illustrated by Mary Azarian, HMH/Houghton 2009, ages 6-9, 48 pages

Darwin and Evolution for Kids: His Life and Ideas with 21 Activities by Kristan Lawson, Chicago Review Press 2003, ages 9-12, 146 pages

Inside the Beagle with Charles Darwin by Fiona Macdonald and Mark Bergin, Enchanted Lion Books 2005, ages 9-12, 48 pages

One Beetle Too Many: The Extraordinary Adventures of Charles Darwin by Kathryn Lasky, illustrated by Matthew Trueman, Candlewick 2009, ages 7-12, 48 pages

On the Origin of Species: The Illustrated Edition by Charles Darwin, edited by David Quammen, Sterling 2008, ages 10-up, 560 pages

Origin: The Story of Charles Darwin by Bruno Leone, Morgan Reynolds Publishing 2009, YA, 160 pages

The Tree of Life: Charles Darwin by Peter Sís, Farrar, Straus and Giroux 2003, ages 9-12, 48 pages

The True Adventures of Charley Darwin by Carolyn Meyer, historical fiction, HMH/Harcourt 2009, ages 12-up, 336 pages

What Darwin Saw: The Journey That Changed the World by Rosalyn Schanzer, National Geographic 2009, ages 10-13, 48 pages

What Mr. Darwin Saw by Mick Manning and Brita Ganström, a graphic novel account of the voyage, Frances Lincoln 2009, ages 6-9, 48 pages

Who Was Charles Darwin? by Deborah Hopkinson, illustrated by Nancy Harrison, Grosset & Dunlap 2005, ages 9-12, 112 pages

Young Charles Darwin and the Voyage of the Beagle by Ruth Ashby, Peachtree 2009, ages 7-10, 128 pages

INDEX

A

Albemarle Island, 76
*American Dictionary of the English
    Language* (Webster), 12
Andersen, Hans Christian, 86
Andes Mountains, 68–70
Arabian Nights, 100
armadillo, 47
Athenaeum Club, 84
Audubon, John James, 14, 15
Austen, Jane, 9

B

Bahia, 36
Basket, Fuegia, 40–50
Beagle (ship), 26–27, 32–33
Beaufort, Francis, 67
Birds of North America
    (Audubon), 15
Blondin, Charles, 99
boobies, 72
Braid, James, 93
Brodie, Jessie, 100
Brontë, Charlotte, 93
Brothers Grimm, 9
Burke, William, 12
Button, Jemmy, 49–50

C

Cambridge Philosophical Society,
    82
Cape Town, South Africa, 79
capybara, 45
Chatham Island, 76
Chopin, Frederic, 12
Christmas Carol, A (Dickens), 93
Church Missionary Society, 49

Corfield, Richard, 64
Covington, Syms, 55, 64
Curig, Capel, 25
curiosity cabinets, 3

D

D'Orbigny, Alcide, 59
daisy trees, 76
Darwin's finches, 75, 83
Darwin, Anne Elizabeth:
    birth of, 92;
    sickness and death of, 105–107
Darwin, Charles. *See also*
    Evolution: arguments for
    marriage, 90;
    birth of, 1;
    collections of, 3, 17;
    death of, 118;
    early education of, 7–8;
    family code names, 4;
    higher education of, 11;
    marriage proposal of, 89;
    mother's death, 6;
    notebooks of, 36;
    opposition to slavery, 37;
    passion for hunting, 9;
    theology and, 16–17;
    tin ear of, 18;
    writing process of, 114
Darwin, Charles Waring:
    birth of, 110;
    birth of, 97;
    sickness and death of, 110
Darwin, Erasmus, 1, 4;
    as abolitionist, 37
Darwin, Henrietta "Etty," 94
Darwin, Horace, 97

Darwin, Leonard, 97
Darwin, Mary Eleanor, 94
Darwin, Susannah Wedgewood, 1
Darwin, William Erasmus, 91
David Copperfield (Dickens), 99
Descent of Man (Darwin), 113, 118
Dickens, Charles, 86
Douglass, Frederick, 86
Down House, 94, 113

E

Earle, Augustus, 39, 58
Edmonstone, John, 12
Einstein, Albert, 121
El Pico del Teide, 22
Erie Canal, 12
*Essay on the Principle of
    Population* (Malthus), 87, 109
evolution. *See* Darwin, Charles:
    as attack on religion, 94;
    Christian Fundamentalism
        and, 120;
    early ideas of, 5;
    theory of, 116
Eyre, Jane, 93

F

Falkland Islands, 61–62
Fernandez, Juan, 67
fireflies, 41
Fitzroy, Robert, 27–28. *See also*
    Beagle (ship)
Fox, William Darwin, 17
Frankenstein (Shelley), 9
Franklin, Benjamin, 2
Fulton, Robert, 1

G
Galapagos iguanas, 74
Galapagos Islands, 71–77
Galapagos penguins, 72
Galapagos tortoises, 72–73
Gould, John, 59, 75, 83
Grant, Robert, 13
guanacos, 59
Gulliver's Travels, 100
Gully, James Manby, 102

H
Hare, William, 12
Hawthorne, Nathaniel, 99
Henslow, John Stevens, 19, 82
Herschel, John, 79–80, 113
Homo erectus, 85
Homo neandertalensis, 85
Homo sapiens, 85
Hooker, Joseph, 100, 110
Hope, Thomas Charles, 12
Huxley, Thomas H., 115

I
Illustrations of British Insects, 18
Industrial Revolution, 1
Intelligent Design, 121
Introduction to the Study of Natural Philosophy (Herschel), 21
Irving, Washington, 1
Isle of Wight, 112

J
Jackson, Andrew, 86
Jameson, Robert, 13
Jenny the orangutan, 92
Journal and Remarks (Darwin), 84

K
King, Philip Gidley, 30, 39
Kingsley, Charles, 115

L
Lamarck, Jean-Baptiste, 5
Last of the Mohicans, The, 100
Leaves of Grass (Whitman), 99
Lincoln, Abraham, 1
Linnaeus, Carolus, 85
Linnean Society, The, 110–111
Lunar Society, 1
Lyell, Charles, 67, 82, 109
"Lunaticks," 1. *See also* Lunar Society

M
Macaw Cottage, 91
Macintosh, Charles, 12
Malthus, Thomas, 87
marriages: between cousins, 91
Matthews, Richard, 52
Megatherium, 54
Minster, York, 49–50
Moby Dick (Melville), 99
mockingbirds, 77
monkey laws, 120

N
natural selection, 87–88
Natural Selection (Darwin), 108

O
Old Curiosity Shop, The, 93
Oliver Twist (Dickens), 86
On the Origin of Species (Darwin), 84, 99, 115
Owen, Richard, 47, 85

P
Personal Narrative (Humboldt), 21
planaria, 41
Plinian Society, 13
Pride and Prejudice (Austen), 9
Principles of Geology (Lyell), 30
professional science: beginning of, 21
Puna, 69

R
Roosevelt, Theodore, 2

S
Scarlet Letter, The (Hawthorne), 99
scientific creationism, 120–121
Scopes, John, 120
seashells: in Valparaiso, 64
Sedgwick, Adam, 21, 24, 82
Shelly, Mary Wollstonecraft, 9
Singer, Isaac, 99
slavery: Darwin's opposition to, 37
Smith, John, 52
South American rhea, 45–46, 86
species, stability of, 81. *See also* evolution
Steinway, Henry, 99
Stokes, John Lort, 30
Stowe, Harriet Beecher, 99

T
Taglioni, 97
Tenerife, 22–23
Tennyson, Alfred, 24
theory of relativity, 121
Thoreau, Henry David, 99
Thorley, Catherine, 100
Tierra Del Fuego, 49